The Conservative Mind:

From Burke to Eliot

Russell Kirk

Russell Kirk's "The Conservative Mind"
abridged by **Aaron McLeod**

Copyright October 2005 by the Alabama Policy Institute
Birmingham, Alabama

Nothing contained herein should be construed as an effort
to aid or hinder any legislation.

About This Series

The Alabama Policy Institute commissioned "Essential Readings for the Modern Conservative" to provide busy conservative-minded individuals with a way to acquaint themselves with at least the rudiments of conservatism. A 500-plus page work like Russell Kirk's *The Conservative Mind,* the first of this series, might seem too large to be worked into the corners of our schedule, but a condensed version could be read in a weekend or on a long flight. With such an abridged version, conservatives of all educational levels will be able to read swiftly and concisely what the best minds in American conservative thought have had to say. This series is an attempt to capture the central message of the various authors and to express it in fewer, simpler words. We believe there are still men and women in sufficient numbers today who take their values seriously and who consider themselves to be of conservative principle but might be hard pressed to explain their political philosophy. This series is for them.

It is certainly true that these condensations were written in hopes of providing a rough familiarity with the ideas of leading conservative thinkers, but they were also written to whet the appetite enough to motivate the reader to tackle the main text as well. It is the nature of a summary to touch upon the main points of a text and omit the full beauty of the original prose; all of the illustrations and the humor — the personality of the author, must be left behind in the primary source. These smaller versions of great works are far better reading than nothing at all, but who is satisfied with the appetizer when he can have the main course?

TABLE OF CONTENTS

Chapter One
The Idea of Conservatism

Russell Kirk was a pillar of American intellectual conservatism. Willmoore Kendall called him "the benevolent sage of Mecosta," and so he was, producing one erudite work after another at Piety Hill, his ancestral home in rural Michigan. Chief among his works is *The Conservative Mind*, his doctoral dissertation for St. Andrews and conservatism's most highly regarded resource for heritage and scholarly authority. First published in 1953 and revised six times since, this thick volume did more than most to provide a genealogy of ideas for the fledgling conservative renaissance that followed World War II. In this *magnum opus*, Kirk traces the history of modern conservatism through its leading lights, beginning with British statesman Edmund Burke and concluding, in the revised edition, with literary critic T.S. Eliot. Kirk surveys the great names of Anglo-American conservative thought and gleans lessons as fresh today as when he first taught them. Even in such diverse figures as John Adams, John C. Calhoun, and Samuel Taylor Coleridge, Kirk finds common strands of thought that can provide forceful, much-needed answers to the perennial question: What is conservatism?

Kirk's work of 509 pages is divided into 13 chapters, 11 of which are devoted to examinations of the men he believed represented, to varying degree, conservative ideas in their time. His first chapter is an excellent introduction to the rest of the book because in it Kirk reveals what he considers to be the essence of conservatism. To make sense of his choices among the literary and political leaders of the past requires that we know his guide rule, and while Kirk is careful to call his work an extended essay in definition, he provides six canons, or rules, into which he thinks Anglo-American conservatism can be distilled. Over his own reluctance to give any list resembling "a fixed and immutable body of dogmata," Kirk identifies the following six characteristics as belonging to a true conservative:

- Belief in a transcendent order or body of natural law that rules society as well as conscience. There is objective truth in the universe, and we can know it. Further, it is the great object of politics to apprehend and apply true Justice to a "community of souls." Kirk rightly places this idea first on the list; for a conservative, moral relativism is not an option. On this point all others will depend. There *are* such things as truth and right, falsehood and wrong. Without an unchanging standard, attempts at social living are doomed beforehand for failing to acknowledge that men are spiritual beings not infinitely malleable.

- Affection for the variety and mystery of human existence, as opposed to the narrow uniformity and egalitarianism of "radical" systems. Conservatives are convinced that life is worth living, as Kirk was fond of saying, and, unlike liberals, do not seek to force sameness upon humanity.

- Conviction that civilized society needs the rule of law and the middle class, in contrast to the notion of a "classless society." Conservatives believe there are natural distinctions among men, leading to inequalities of condition. Conservatives affirm equality before God and the courts; anything more leads to "servitude and boredom."

- Freedom and property are linked: without private property, the state is unstoppable. Redistribution of wealth, by taxes or other means, is not economic progress. Men need property to secure their rights, discharge their duties, and limit government.

- Faith in prescription and distrust of those calculating men who would reconstruct all of society according to their own abstract designs. A conservative believes things are the way they are for a good reason: past generations have passed on customs and conventions that stood the test of time. Customs serve as a check on anarchy and the lust for power.

- Recognition that change may not be a good thing. Hasty innovation can destroy as well as improve, so conservatives are prudent with their changes and approach reform with caution rather than zeal.

Kirk allows that deviations from this list have occurred, as well as additions to it. But, most conservatives of the last two centuries have adhered to these canons "with some consistency." Kirk does a fine job of demonstrating how each of the men he examines, manifested these principles.

Kirk makes a brief attempt at identifying key principles of liberal thought, as well, in his first chapter. The belief in man's perfectibility, contempt for tradition, political leveling, and economic leveling, with a secular view of the state's origins perhaps thrown in, serve as well as can be expected to identify the radicals in our midst. Kirk slaps them with what is for him a searing indictment: they are in love with change.

Chapter Two
Burke and the Politics of Prescription

In this chapter, Kirk lavishes attention on the father of modern conservatism in the British-American tradition: Edmund Burke, the Irishman who served his beloved Britain with fervor prior to and during the French Revolution. He was a member of the Whig Party, and as such he stood for checks on governmental power, religious tolerance, and limits on imperial expansion abroad. Burke was an opponent of arbitrary power wherever he saw it encroaching and was equally ready to defend both the monarchy and the English Constitution against Parliament.

Burke believed reform was inevitable and could be a good thing, but he knew the liberties Englishmen enjoyed were the fruits of a deliberate and painstaking process that took generations to establish. Reform, then, needed to be cautious, reverent, and prudent, or else it might destroy where it ought to improve. Burke had cause to be nervous. Across the English Channel, the heads of state were quite literally being cut from their French shoulders. Burke was horrified at the blood and chaos that came spewing out of the Continent after 1789. His best-known work by far is his *Reflections on the Revolution in France,* a work Kirk credits as being that to which "philosophical conservatism owes its being."[1] Burke had to fight hard to safeguard the British system from the sort of root-and-branch upheaval he saw under the Jacobins. With *Reflections*, Burke sounded the alarm for his fellow Britons, alerting them that if the consuming zeal for "liberty, equality, fraternity" was not quenched at home, the fires of destruction would swim the Channel and set all England ablaze.

Kirk devotes the second section of his second chapter to Burke's writings against the British and French radicals of his time in *An Appeal from the New to the Old Whigs, A Letter to a Noble Lord,* and *Thoughts on a Regicide Peace,* in addition to *Reflections.* Kirk calls these combined works the charter of conservatism, for with them by 1793 Burke succeeded in checking the enthusiasm for French innovation and social leveling that were encroaching on Britain.

In replying to the arguments of the *philosophes* who led the intellectual movement that produced the Reign of Terror, Burke had no choice but to enter a realm he generally detested—metaphysical abstraction. Burke was a man of particulars, of the concrete, and of the real. He believed the arid world of abstract theory so beloved by the radicals was a danger to the real liberties of Englishmen. Nevertheless, in his responses to men such as Rousseau and Bentham and their tenets, Burke framed a triumphant philosophy of conservatism on the belief that first principles in the moral sphere come to us through revelation

tion and intuition, not the fanciful speculations of dreamy philosophers. By the advent of World War I and the Russian Revolution, Kirk notes that the classical liberals of Burke's day, like Acton, were proved wrong in their criticism that Burke overreacted to the French Revolution.

Kirk spends the third section of the chapter discussing Burke's religious views, which are foundational to the ideals of conservatism. According to Burke, if we are to know the state, we must first know the man as a spiritual being.

Burke saw society as a creation of Divine providence. God's will for political man is known "through the prejudices and traditions which millennia of human experience with divine means and judgments have implanted in the mind of the species,"[2] and so arrogant faith in frail human reason deserves scorn. The hand of God has moved slowly and subtly in the history of many generations, guiding, allowing, and restraining. To Burke, it was impious for man to elevate his isolated intellect against the collected wisdom of human history and plan a utopia built to his specifications. His belief in the sinfulness of human nature, a hallmark of conservatism, made him an implacable enemy of those who attempt to craft heaven on earth. Unlike the thinkers of the Enlightenment, Burke was unwilling to dismiss discussions of first principles and moral philosophy. For him, either we are sinful creatures, made by God but fallen, or we are adrift in a moral vacuum, subject to the whims of the strongest. The following quotation of Burke's best sums up his views:

> Taking it for granted that I do not write to the disciples of the Parisian philosophy, I may assume, that the awful Author of our being is the author of our place in the order of existence; and that having disposed and marshalled us by a divine tactic, not according to our will, but according to His, He has, in and by that disposition, virtually subjected us to act the part which belongs to the part assigned to us. We have obligations to mankind at large, which are not in consequence of any special voluntary pact. They arise from the relation of man to man, and the relation of man to God, which relations are not a matter of choice. . . . When we marry, the choice is voluntary, but the duties are not a matter of choice. . . . The instincts which give rise to this mysterious process of nature are not of our making. But out of physical causes, unknown to us, perhaps unknowable, arise moral duties, which, as we are able perfectly to comprehend, we are bound indispensably to perform.[3]

Burke's piety is evidently linked to his political philosophy. For him, statesmen were far more than representatives of the people, elected to do their bidding; their tasks are sacred, their offices consecrated to the betterment of future generations and the observance of immortal truth. Especially in popular government, Kirk notes, a sense of holy purpose is needful—the people need to understand their responsibility in holding power. For Burke, society was a sacred thing, a tacit agreement between the dead, the living, and the yet unborn, to be protected and nurtured for ends that do not all bring immediate gain. And, if society is sacred, if the world is ordered according to a divine plan, we ought to tinker with it only in fear and trembling. Burke, Kirk informs us, "could not conceive of a durable social order without the spirit of piety."[4]

To sustain such a spirit, Burke relied on the national church and its influence in British culture. The church must consecrate public office and instill veneration for the world as God has given it to us. Church and state, far from being separate entities in Burke's eyes, were dependent on each other, after a fashion. While the church may not need the state to survive, the state surely needs the church, for, as Kirk put it, "true religion is not merely an expression of national spirit; it rises far superior to earthly law, being, indeed, the source of all law."[5]

In section four of this chapter, Kirk turns to Burke's thinking on the role and significance of prescription, tradition, and custom to the preservation of the social order. Burke, he writes, had to answer the following questions: What is the foundation of authority in politics? How may men judge the prudence and justice of any particular act? The supernatural realm does not micromanage the routine details of earthly life, so where are men to look for guidance on political judgments? Burke had an answer: the collective wisdom of mankind through millennia of experience and meditation, taught by Providence—in other words, tradition. Man ought to have respect in his everyday decisions for the customs and laws of mankind and apply them with expediency.

Tradition enables men to live together with some degree of peace; it manages to direct consciences and check the appetites. Kirk quotes Burke on this point, writing "Somewhere there must be a control upon will and the appetite; and the less of it there is within, the more of it there must be without."[6] Burke did not trust reason to keep most men in line, for most men, he suspected, did not employ the rational faculty at all, and those who tried often did so without sufficient education. He would rather trust common sense and the wisdom of ancient custom to guide the masses and restrain their more base appetites. Were the "crust" of prejudice and prescription to crack, civilization would shudder on its foundations. If men began altering the constitution of their state whenever they wanted, no generation would link with another. In Burke's powerful phrase, "men would become no better than the flies of a summer."[7]

Did Burke expect men to resist all temptation to change, then? Far from it—properly guided, change is a process of renewal. Burkean change is a slow, loving process of patching and polishing the old order of things, in Kirk's words, "allowing natural processes to take their course while cooling the heels of those infatuated with instant reform." The best reformer, to Kirk, is one who "combines an ability to reform with a disposition to preserve; the man who loves change is wholly disqualified, from his lust, to be the agent of change."[8]

For his fifth section on Burke, Kirk surveys the statesman's thinking on a contentious issue of his day: natural rights. Burke rejected the Enlightenment doctrine of the natural rights of man, including Locke's and Rousseau's teachings. Burke looked back to an older tradition, to the *ius naturale* (natural law) of Cicero, reinforced by Christian dogma and English common law. Man's rights had not to do with what was owed *him*, but rather what *man* owed his Maker. Burke, rejecting the above figures as well as the teachings of Hume and Bentham, instead defined natural right as human custom conforming to divine intent. He denounced the idea of an idyllic, free state of nature, from which man voluntarily came into society, there to critique its laws by the rights he supposedly had beforehand. Neither history nor tradition sustains the idea of a primeval paradise such as the *philosophes* posited. Instead we must muddle along as best we can, seeking to conform our laws to those of God, recognizing our limitations and respecting the prescriptive rights handed down by our forebears. We have rights, to be sure, but Burke saw nothing but danger in attempting to judge what he called the chartered rights of civilized men by an abstracted notion of the rights of primitive man. Social man has given up any claim to absolute autonomy to gain a measure of peace and security; and to the benefits of that society man does have a right, but that right must be defined by convention, and by august tradition. Burke believed men could claim a right to equality before the law, security of labor and property, civilized institutions, and order. These are the purposes for which God ordained the state; these are the real rights of man, confirmed by custom and upheld by law.

Social and political equality, however, were not among what Burke considered to be man's real natural rights. Instead, he believed that aristocracy and hierarchy were natural, and in the sixth section of this chapter, Kirk observes how Burke understands equality. Is there a sort of equality with which God has endowed us? Yes, Burke replies, though only one sort: moral equality. Men are judged fairly by their Creator; no man has more innate value as a human being than any other. As for every other measurement, such as wealth, birth, intelligence, and beauty, we are unequal.

Men are largely unequal in the ways of political authority. Certainly political equality is an artificial product; men have no natural right to majority rule, because not all men are born with what Burke believed to be the necessary qualifications (education, moral nature, tradition, property). Burke feared the results of a government controlled by an omnicompetent majority, as Kirk quotes him, "The will of the many, and their *interest*, must very often differ; and great will be the difference when they make an evil choice."[9]

We have come a long way since Burke; in many countries, such as ours, there is nearly universal adulthood suffrage. The point to learn from Burke is that such widespread political power is the result of expediency, not moral argument. There is no natural law of equality, but it is awfully hard to convince men of why they should not be able to vote once they see their neighbors voting. Kirk puts the case as follows: "political equality is therefore in some sense unnatural, Burke concludes; and aristocracy, on the other hand, is in a certain sense natural."[10] Despite his reservations, Burke believed that nature had provided society with the materials for an aristocracy that could produce competent leadership. Burke respected high birth, to be sure, but he had in mind a different sort of aristocracy. In one of his most memorable passages, he explains,

> To be bred in a place of estimation; to see nothing low and sordid from one's infancy; to be taught to respect one's self; to be habituated to the censorial inspection of the public eye; to look early to public opinion; to stand upon such elevated ground as to be enabled to take a large view of the wide-spread and infinitely diversified combinations of men and affairs in a large society; to have leisure to read, to reflect, to converse; to be enabled to draw the court and attention of the wise and learned wherever they are to be found; to be habituated in the pursuit of honour and duty; to be formed to the highest degree of vigilance, foresight, and circumspection, in a state of things in which no fault is committed with impunity, and the slightest mistakes draw on the most ruinous consequences; to be led to a guarded and regulated conduct, from a sense that you are considered as an instructor of your fellow-citizens in their highest concerns, and that you act as a reconciler between God and man; to be employed as an administrator of law and justice, and to be thereby amongst the first benefactors to mankind; to be a professor of high science, or of liberal and ingenious art; to be amongst rich traders, who from their success are presumed to have sharp and vigorous understandings, and to possess the virtues of diligence, order, constancy, and regularity, and to have cultivated an habitual regard to commutative justice—these are the circumstances of men, that form what I should call a *natural* aristocracy, without which there is no nation.[11]

organized in this fashion would conform to the eternal natural order that holds all things in place. A government that cooperates with the created order ensures the vitality of civil society. We adapt and trim and prune the old order to deal with new circumstances, but we do not seek to reconstruct our way of life to suit revolutionary abstractions. Burke's understanding of nature and rights, of permanence and change, writes Kirk, "lift[s] Burke to a plane of reflection far above the simple postulates of French reforming speculation, and give his ideas an enduring elevation superior to the vicissitudes of politics."[12]

Perhaps the greatest monument to Burke's brilliance and moral leadership was that there was no English Revolution in the late 18th century. Unlike France, he succeeded in keeping Jacobinism from sweeping Britain. He founded a school of politics on the concepts of prudence and veneration for the past, a school that has ever since fought the appetite for innovation. Kirk sums up his praise for the statesman in his seventh and last section by saying, "his reverence for the wisdom of our ancestors, through which works the design of Providence, is the first principle of all consistent conservative thought."[13]

Chapter Three
John Adams and Liberty Under Law

In his third chapter, Kirk moves across the Atlantic to consider early American exemplars of conservatism. Kirk identifies the greatest of these as John Adams, whom he names the founder of true conservatism in America. Adams was responsible, more than anyone else, for keeping the American government one of laws, not men.

Kirk also considers other men first, men such as Alexander Hamilton and Fisher Ames, Federalists who sought to preserve the best of the British order in the newly-independent nation and who resisted the efforts of Jeffersonian Republicans to produce wholesale change. Kirk calls their party the "anti-democratic, property-respecting, centralizing, rather short-sighted Federalism,"[14] to which Adams often was superior. Hamilton and Ames were more "orthodox" in their Federalism than Adams, and to them we turn.

With *The Federalist Papers*, Alexander Hamilton established himself as one of the most influential expositors of the U.S. Constitution. His political principles, says Kirk, were simple: he was suspicious of local or popular impulses and believed security from a leveling influence lay in a firm national authority. America would not have a unitary central government, so he settled for a federal one, energetically advocating for it with his contributions to "The Federalist" and other pamphlets. According to Kirk, though, his idealism had its flaws. It apparently never occurred to Hamilton that a centralized government could be a leveling and innovating government, nor did he bet on the social changes brought about by the industrialization of the North that he desired. Hamilton was a practical man of great ability, but those abilities, Kirk tells us, "had for their substratum a set of traditional assumptions almost naïve; and he rarely speculated upon what compound might result from mixing his prejudices with the elixir of American industrial vigor."[15] Hamilton did not anticipate the stubbornness of the state and local governments in resisting the centralization of power. He thought his program for a strong national government would eventually eliminate these obstacles "by provoking a civil war which did more than all of Jefferson's speculations to dissipate the tranquil eighteenth-century aristocratic society that really was Hamilton's aspiration."[16] Kirk sees Hamilton as well-intentioned but inadequate to the task he set for himself. He was a man of particulars, who never penetrated far beneath the political surface to the "mysteries of veneration and presumption."[17]

Kirk dedicates the third section of this chapter to Fisher Ames, a sour fellow from Dedham, Massachusetts. Ames, while possessing a mastery of literary style, never had much impact on the events of his day. He had already given up the fight. His conservatism was of the purely reactionary sort which, never admitting change, perishes where it stands. Ames was pessimistic about the American experiment because he doubted there were sufficient numbers of men with the moral courage and charisma to preserve the country from the passions of the multitudes and the demagogues who master them. He was convinced that the people as a body cannot reason and are easily swayed by clever speakers and political agents. In his words, "few can reason, all can feel. . . ."[18] Democracy could not last, Ames thundered, "for despotism lies at the door; when the tyranny of the majority leads to chaos, society will submit to rule by the sword."[19]

To Ames, what doomed the American experiment was the democratic destruction of morals. Because nothing stood in the way of popular rule, Ames believed that justice and morality in America would fail, and popular rule cannot support justice, without which moral habits fall away. Neither the free press nor paper constitutions could safeguard order from these excesses, for the first is merely a stimulus to popular passion and imagination, while the other is a thin bulwark against corruption. When old prescription and tradition are dismissed, only naked force matters. Of American prospects, Ames said in despair, "to mitigate a tyranny, is all that is left for our hopes."[20]

Thankfully, Ames was wrong. Though the pending War of 1812 and the death of the Federalist Party made for a bleak future, already there were countervailing forces to be found in the moderating tendency of the agrarian society Jefferson represented and the sober practicality of the Adamses, John and John Quincy. Regrettably, Ames never saw these; in 1807 he "shrugged his shoulders, and turned to the wall. . . ."[21]

Kirk paints a much brighter picture in his fourth section, for there he takes up the central figure of the chapter, John Adams, "the real conservative.[22] Like Burke, Adams detested the fanaticism and speculation of the French Revolution and wrote his *Defence of the Constitutions* to counteract their notions of liberty and hopefully influence the delegates to the Constitutional Convention. Kirk draws similarities between Adams and Burke, but where Burke spoke of prejudice, prescription, and natural rights, Adams attacked the twin doctrines of human perfectibility and the unified state. Kirk splits his treatment of Adams along these lines.

First, Kirk examines Adams' thought on human nature. Adams particularly targeted Condorcet, a member of the French Enlightenment, for what he saw as the Frenchman's inexcusably high opinion of human character. While Adams was a firm believer in the fallen nature of man and the danger of unchecked passions, Condorcet believed in equality of condition for all and rejected the notion that man's flaws could not be overcome by the right legislation and institutions. Adams did believe in progress, in amelioration of the human condition, but he warned that "wild snatches at perfection" *à la* Condorcet or Rousseau would ruin real advancement. Adams also ruled out the common quick fix forwarded by such radicals: education. Once a schoolmaster himself, he sneered at the idea that man is perfect in "nature" and only corrupted by exposure to knowledge and civilization. He knew formal education would only make man more clever, not better. Kirk continues for Adams, writing,

> We cannot expect formal education radically to alter the common impulses of the heart; only the much more difficult inculcation of morality, which comes from the snail-slow influence of historical example and just constitutions rather than from deliberate legislation, can effect [sic] that moral improvement which is the real progress of humanity.[23]

As Kirk notes, there is much of life not to be gotten out of schools. A conscience cannot be formed through a library. The struggles and pains of life common to all will not be eliminated by philosophers or legislators, though they may be made worse in the attempt. According to Adams, the drive to perfect man will end in his abolition.[24]

In Kirk's fifth section we learn that Adams also excoriated the French speculators not only for their infatuation with human perfectibility, but also for their love of equality. Adams insisted that, far from all men being substantially equal, there actually is a natural aristocracy of men, formed from the benefactors of the unavoidable inequality of humankind. Like Burke, Adams held to every man having equal rights to his own and equal standing before God. Beyond that, though, men are unequal in their powers and faculties, influence in society, property and advantages, piety and iniquity, and nearly every other attribute. Especially in his letters to John Taylor of Caroline, Adams drove home his conviction of the natural inequality of men.

Kirk warns that Adams' theory of the natural aristocracy is one of the most misinterpreted and distorted opinions Adams ever shared. Adams' understanding of it was simple: any man who can influence others to vote as he would have them is an aristocrat and a leader. He is called a *natural* aristocrat because he is not created by society. He has no titles, no legal privileges; he is who he is because he was born that way. Positive law cannot destroy such an aristocracy and is not necessary for its existence. Kirk points out that Adams is not really defending the concept as much as indicating its existence. Natural aristocracy is a phenomenon of nature regardless of whether we like it.

Adams turns next, in Kirk's sixth section, to determine what manner of government best accommodates this fact. Happiness is the end of government, says Adams, but man's happiness consists in virtue. A man must first be good to be happy. Adams preferred to speak of virtue rather than of freedom or liberty, though he did not think them mutually exclusive. Instead of liberty being created by fiat, it must be the creation of civilization and "heroic exertions by a few brave souls."[25] To that end, Adams outlined a practical system for liberty under law, for under law liberty must be, else it will survive only, in Kirk's phrase, "as a lamb among wolves."[26]

Adams finds that the form of government that will best nurture the public and private virtue crucial to an ordered liberty is a republic. And not just any sort of a republic, since both an aristocracy and a democracy in their pure forms are hostile to liberty. Adams advocated for a republic in which power was separated, with different branches of government checking each other.

Turgot, a French financier and Adams' target for the arguments made in his *Constitutions*, disparaged the Americans' new state constitutions for having followed Montesquieu's advice on subjecting liberty to law. Turgot would have had liberty as an absolute value with the "general will" allowing direct rule by majority will. What he wanted was simplicity in government, something Adams knew to be a grave danger. Uniformity and unity in power is the road to despotism, as the progress of the French Revolution amply demonstrated. Burke and Adams alike shuddered at this lust after simplicity. Adams would have heartily agreed when Burke said, "When I hear the simplicity of contrivance aimed at, and boasted of, in any new political constitution, I am at no loss to decide that the artificers are grossly ignorant of their trade, and totally ignorant of their duty."[27] Adams knew that a balanced system of split powers would force government to make decisions by deliberation and consensus, which would "beget moderation" and temper the exercise of power. In his *Constitutions*, Adams surveys many varied states and forms of government with overwhelming erudition, all to persuade whoever would listen that three separate branches of government, a balance of powers, is truly necessary for free men to possess their liberty in peace.

In his seventh and last section, Kirk mentions that great monument of the Federalists, the most conservative device in the history of the world: The United States Constitution. He reminds us that Chief Justice John Marshall, a Federalist to the core, accomplished more while on the bench, in practical terms, than did either Adams or Hamilton. Marshall made the Court the arbiter of the Constitution and made the Constitution the "incarnation of Federalistic conservatism."[28] Though he swam against the tide of the Administration and Congress, Marshall's decisions became law, showing the turn of the tide for Federalist arguments. The party was defunct, but the ideas of Federalist conservatism came to master the national consciousness, and that influence, the heritage of men like Adams, has endured to this day.

Chapter Four
Romantics and Utilitarians

After looking at the man who saved Britain from Jacobin chaos, and after survey-ing a few who sailed the turbulent waters of the American founding, Kirk travels back across the Atlantic to Burke's homeland and acquaints us with the 19th-century battle between the Romantics and the Utilitarians. He finds three men worthy of mention, con-servatives who strove to break the looming wave of change and upheaval before it deluged their country. First in line is the estimable Scottish novelist, Sir Walter Scott.

Romantics like Scott, Coleridge, and Wordsworth knew the Utilitarian philosophy of Jeremy Bentham as their mortal enemy. Benthamite doctrines, they perceived, posed grave threats to the past, to the variety of life, to tradition, to custom and beauty, and so they sought to restrain what Kirk calls the "intolerant new industrial secularism" Bentham brought with him. Bentham's ideas swept England with radical changes that reflected and encouraged the growth of industrial production and the rise of the masses to power. His great test was *utility*, which, Kirk says, being empty of higher imagination and ignorant of the spiritual nature of man, reduced the merit of an act to a mathematical ratio of pleasure and pain. Bentham assumed if men were only shown how to solve such an equation, they would be good, and once the majority had direct control of government, politics would be essentially a thing of the past.

Burke could have agreed with Bentham that society as the end is the greatest good for the greatest number, but he would have meant something altogether different by it. Burke believed man's good meant conformity to the Author of his being and His estab-lished order, a life of piety, of duty, and of love. Kirk accuses Bentham of sweeping that aside, in favor of a reconstruction of society to bring about as much political equality as possible and so allow the will of the majority to hold uncontested sway.

Bentham's moral and political system has been tossed into the dustbin of history, Kirk assures us, but his legal reforms still plague us. Of Utilitarian legal theory Kirk writes,

> Men should make and unmake their laws, Bentham thought, upon the prin-ciple of utility; law ought to be treated like mathematics or physics, made a tool of convenience; the old illusion that law had a supernatural sanction, an origin superior to man, the Ciceronian and Scholastic notion that it was a human groping after divine enactment, should be dismissed in the inter-est of efficiency in an industrial age.[29]

It was on this issue of legal reform that Scott contended with the followers of Bentham; Scott stood with Burke in refusing to swallow the idea that any body of men, whether a majority or not, has the right to make any law they pleased. Scott knew law must have a higher sanction than numbers to preserve the order and liberty of human society, and he put forth all his power as novelist and poet to impede Bentham's ruinous legal novelty.

Scott was the heart of the Romantic movement; he succeeded in popularizing with literary aplomb the doctrines of Burkean conservatism. Scott's *Waverly* novels far exceeded Burke's *Reflections* in their sales, reaching a great many people otherwise inaccessible to such ideas. He painted with vivid imagery the worth of tradition, the value of the little societies and local customs that were the pride of his beloved Scotland. He made the thought of Burke a "living and tender thing," writes Kirk, and showed how reverence for our forefathers and compliance with our duties, acceptance and appreciation of the "unbought grace of life," form the foundations of civilized moral order.[30]

Like Scott, British Prime Minister George Canning believed in the complexity and variety of the human experience; like Scott, he fought against the Jacobin drive to homogenize society. Section two of this chapter is devoted to the bright but short-lived star of Canning's rise to power on the shoulders of the Tory party. Young Canning, an energetic and imaginative leader, began his political career as a Whig and thus owed nothing to the older Tory lineage from Bolingbroke and the Cavaliers; his conservatism began, writes Kirk, with the French Revolution. His leadership potential lay in the fact that, unlike his fellow Tories, he was capable of applying the principles of conservatism, which he derived from Burke, to his own "epoch of change." Sadly, it was this distinction from his peers that would lead to their failure to support him in his hour of need. Kirk notes that the Tory party had been wracked by fear for a generation and trembled at the mention of innovation. When Canning, with his "flashing sagacity," came on the scene, his conservative bona fides notwithstanding, the timid Tories declined to place their faith in this charismatic and ambitious man. Kirk explains, "The great Tory proprietors, thinking of his shabby boyhood and his arrogant aspirations, wondered if they dared entrust their defenses to an adventurer...and the manufacturing and trading interest...dreaded his boldness."[31]

As a result, they doomed their own party. Canning was prime minister for a mere four months, and while he had worked miracles as foreign secretary, as the head of government he accomplished almost nothing. He was deserted by the Tories as soon as he began to form his administration; Kirk ventures that it was the strain of attempting to drag his party after him that caused his early death.

For a man who accomplished little, though, he did this much: he set a powerful example for future generations, and Kirk speculates on what he could have and would have done if his supporters had stood with him, writing,

> The Old Tories failed him at the moment when he might have rescued them
> from their immobility, because they entertained vague fears that he would
> slide over to liberalism, compromise with the radicals, grant concession
> after concession until Toryism was pared away altogether. They did not
> know him. No statesman was less inclined to accept the compromises of
> uneasy mediocrity or to yield the concessions of timid vacillation. He pro-
> posed to retain all the old framework of the British constitution, but to win
> over, by a vigorous administration, every powerful interest, demonstrating
> how they could find satisfaction within the English tradition. He was
> against parliamentary reform; he saw no need for extension of the suffrage;
> he would have retained the Test and Establishment Acts; he was contemp-
> tuous of all doctrines of abstract right and all utilitarian calculations based
> upon notions of atomic individualism. By efficient government, by admit-
> ting the rights of classes and interests when those influences had become
> clearly entitled to especial consideration, by patching and improving the
> fabric of the state, he intended to preserve the Britain that Burke had
> loved.[32]

Had Canning lived, Kirk maintains, he would have pursued with diligence a course
designed to preserve the beauty of the British order while adapting it to the inevitable
changes coming; he would have, in Kirk's words, "[led] the waters of novelty into the
canals of custom."[33] Alas, it was not to be. William Pitt succeeded Canning as prime minister and gave up far more to the radicals than Canning would have, and the Reform Bill
of 1832, instead of improving the Constitution, admitted vast masses of the populace to
the franchise and abolished ancient boroughs[34] and rights without regard to tradition or
expediency. But, as Kirk puts it, so much for spilt milk. Canning, if he did no more, indi-
cated the best path for conservatives to take in resistance to wholesale innovation and
upheaval. His legacy to conservatism, and the justification for his inclusion in this book,
is that he "instilled in conservatism that suppleness of mind and breadth of purpose which
have enabled the English conservatives to run a tenacious and reasonably consistent
course...longer than any other political party in history."[35]

We go on to the last Romantic Kirk admires in this chapter, the man he calls the
philosopher of the movement, Samuel Taylor Coleridge. John Stuart Mill named
Coleridge and Bentham the two great seminal minds of the 19th century, but where
Bentham's system was built on the rationalism of Locke and the French *philosophes*,

Coleridge, Kirk informs us, "adhered to the Church Fathers and Plato, declaring that full though the eighteenth century had been of enlighteners, it had been terribly empty of enlightenment."[36] Coleridge was convinced that ideas are crucial to the health of society; experience alone cannot suffice as a guide. Principle, not just calculation, is needed to navigate the ship of state. He was a chief force, writes Kirk, in the reinvigoration of British religious conviction after it had suffered from attack by rationalism, and it is good he was, for Coleridge believed moral order and political order depend on each other; without the Idea of the Church, society cannot subsist.

Coleridge's religious conservatism related directly to his social conservatism. He feared that if the Utilitarians were ever successful in undermining the religious consecration of the state, order itself would crumble. If the rationalists made materialists out of the majority of men, misery would ensue. As Kirk puts it, "Men's politics, especially the politics of the busy-body reformer, are contingent upon their religion."[37] Coleridge's religious/political work, *The Constitution of Church and State* (1830), exhibited his conviction that religion and society are not and can never be separate entities, but it was in his *Lay Sermons* of 1817-18 that he systematically expounded his own conservatism, founded upon ideas. His complaint is that the commercial spirit is no longer in balance with the traditional countervailing forces of aristocratic prejudice and orthodox Christianity. Wise reform to meet the changing times must be accompanied by a moral improvement of all the classes of society through Christian education, in the hope that they would be redeemed from greedy materialism; the shape of such an improvement was described in his later work, *The Constitution of the Church and State, According to the Idea of Each* (1830). Coleridge, writing on the ideal form of society, not the British system as it was, argued that the State is "a body politic having the principle of unity within itself,"[38] a unity derived from the interdependence of the great opposite interests, Permanence and Progression. Permanence is his term for the landed interest, the gentry and nobility, and Progression names the commercial and professional classes. These classes are embodied in the two houses of Parliament, with the King as the fulcrum. The third estate is what Coleridge calls the Clerisy, those who serve the Church to cultivate a robust morality in the people and are supported in their work by a portion of the national wealth set aside for them, a portion called the Nationalty. He envisions the clerisy undertaking the education of the public, the dissemination of knowledge and the inculcation of virtue. In symbiotic fashion, the State supports the Church in its task, which, not incidentally, will itself bear up the State.

Such is Coleridge's idea of the Constitution, of which the English system is only an approximation; the path of progress, therefore, is prudent improvement in the direction of the Idea, not subversion of the existing order along radical lines. Coleridge hoped for a nation led by gentlemen and scholars, a nation of balance between the aristocratic class-es and the commercial classes, between the agricultural and the industrial, a nation whose conscience is revived and instructed by a healthy Church of England. As it happened, Coleridge's ideas were ignored by the powers of London; the Reform Bill of 1832 brought radical change in the franchise and the balance of power between the social classes, but it did not provide for the instruction of the newly-empowered merchant classes in morals or political wisdom. A materialistic individualism ruled the uneducated masses, bringing with it the destruction of the antique pieties and institutions of Britain's past. Eventually, however, the Benthamite assumption that enlightened self-interest could replace religious principle ended in a "bitter collectivism," the death knell of Utilitarian liberalism. Conservative thought, Kirk asserts, has outlived it, in part thanks to Coleridge, whose vision inspired the conservative reformers for the next century.

Chapter Five
Southern Conservatism: Randolph and Calhoun

In chapter five Kirk directs our attention to two singular figures in American history. Both of them were staunch in their conservatism and both of them, sadly, are forgotten by many today. In the years preceding the War Between the States, this duo gave their zeal to the cause of the South and its defense from the forces of centralization and industrialization. The elder of the two Kirk takes up first.

John Randolph of Roanoke was, writes Kirk, the architect of Southern conservatism and the prophet of Southern nationalism. Kirk sums up the Southern brand of conservatism into four points: distaste for alteration, a defense of agrarian society, a love for local rights, and sensitivity about "the negro question." For these things Randolph and Calhoun both sacrificed their political careers—Randolph a chance to be Speaker of the House and Calhoun a chance at the presidency. Randolph's fame was in denouncing the democratic tendency to enlarge the sphere of positive law, while Calhoun defended the rights of minorities.

Randolph, writes Kirk, was at once "the terror and delight of Virginia." A lover of freedom, Randolph could not abide the centralizing tenets of Federalism; a great hater of democratic degradation and cant, he castigated Jeffersonianism. Unfortunately, his willingness to denounce both of the strong powers of his time left him almost a man alone. He was supported only by his faithful band of Old Republicans, men, like him, dedicated to strict construction of the Constitution, economy in government, hard money, and peace with the world. His was the only eloquent voice still defending these noble ideals in the era of the non-intercourse acts, Jefferson's Embargo, the War of 1812, and the protective tariffs. This was the era of federal expansion, loose construction, and the National Bank. Only Randolph held forth on behalf of state powers and the old ways—until Calhoun saw the light.

Kirk delights in noting that much of Randolph's conservative wisdom came from Burke; from 1805 onward, Kirk tells us, "Randolph applied to American questions those first principles of politics laid down by the philosopher of conservatism."[39] When he thundered, "change is not reform" in the Virginia Convention of 1829-1830, he spoke with Burke's voice, and like Burke, Randolph was averse to the democratic passion for legislating, believing it to be a danger to liberty. He thought it unwise for Congress to pass laws in the name of justice when prescriptive right, custom, and common law already afforded the real guarantees of liberty. He was convinced that men foolishly imperiled the old prerogatives and freedoms that were the fruit of generations if they insisted on "tinkering" with government, adding and subtracting, regulating and directing after some goal. Positive law lacked the weight and wisdom of prescription and tradition, and men ought not to be trusted with so much arbitrary power. Randolph knew such a lust for innovation in the name of equality or social justice was a front for arbitrary exercise of power. He repudiated the common interpretation of the Declaration of Independence in rejecting the notion of social equality. Kirk observes,

> Men are not born free and equal, said Randolph. Their physical, moral, and intellectual differences are manifest, to say nothing of their difference of birth and wealth. To presume that a mystic "equality" entitles the mass of mankind to tinker at pleasure with society, to play with it as a toy, to exercise their petty ingenuity upon it, is to reduce mankind to the only state of life in which anything resembling equality of condition actually prevails: savagery. Jeffersonian leveling doctrines, if taken literally, mean anarchy, "the chrysalis state of despotism."[40]

Nor did Randolph believe mere parchment, even if it was the Constitution, could alone save us from appetite and force. For him, security was only to be found in continually restricting the scope of government, clearly defining the few objects of government and reserving most of the important powers to the states, as the Founders intended. Freedom for Randolph was specific; it was local. Liberty had to be personal and particular—a man loves his wife, his children, his neighborhood, his community, his state, before he can spare a thought for the nation. Take away a man's liberty in his home, his church, or his town, and you destroy any freedom worth the name. Randolph's conservatism was "the conservatism of particularism, of localism. Without the spirit of particularism, the idea of local associations and local rights, perhaps no sort of conservatism is practicable."[41]

Randolph's second bulwark against tyranny is "common-sense" government. For him, this meant limiting the right to vote to those whose moral character, social standing, and ownership of property "lift them above the temptations of power." Ideally, the men who vote would be the ones with the leisure to reflect on the political issues of the day and thereby make informed decisions, men whose ownership of property gives them a vested interest in defending their rights and those of others to the same, men whose social standing allows them to take a broader view of the state of things than the day laborer.

Common sense also meant exploding the notion that government has some humanitarian responsibility to do for others what they are perfectly capable of doing for themselves. "A more pernicious notion cannot prevail."[42] If the powers of legislating are yielded up to the mass of men, a destructive transfer of private duties to the public burden, in obedience to the doctrines of abstract egalitarianism, will surely follow. Because it flew in the face of common sense, Randolph detested this nanny-state tendency to ease the natural and moral obligations of men by swelling the power of the federal government.

Kirk turns to John C. Calhoun in his third section of the chapter. He describes Calhoun as more reserved, more disciplined than Randolph, if no less firm in his convictions. Unlike his predecessor, Calhoun grew up on the Carolina frontier, without the benefit of a rich library, and unlike Randolph he started life memorizing passages from *The Rights of Man*. He began his political career as a Jeffersonian, a nationalist, and a War Hawk, and had ambitions for the presidency, but his love of freedom eventually won out over his other beliefs; it was this love, Kirk says, that "intervened to convert him into the resolute enemy of national consolidation and of omnicompetent democratic majorities…this principle ruined him as a politician. As a man of thought and a force of history, he was transfigured by it."[43]

Calhoun's first dozen years in politics are passed over by Kirk in favor of the events that changed the course of his career. It was the tariff of 1824 that altered Calhoun's political life. Before its passage, he had truly believed in a benevolent popular reason, a collective good will; with the tariff, though, he saw that reason was malignant, perfectly satisfied with plundering one portion of the country—the South—for the benefit of the congressional majority. He had thought the Constitution, which he dearly loved, a sufficient safeguard against oppression by a class or section of people, but he realized it was not so. Calhoun looked to nullification as a possible remedy to the tyranny of the majority, in this case exercised in the "Tariff of Abominations," but its failure in the controversy with President Andrew Jackson, with disaster averted only by the Clay Compromise, at last convinced him that only power can successfully oppose power.

Calhoun struggled with himself over this problem: how can the rights of minorities be protected by law if a majority can do as it pleases? The Founders had recognized the need for government to protect minorities from a hostile majority and had attempted to provide for that need with strict limitations on federal power and a bill of rights. To Calhoun's eyes, these had not sufficed. He grappled with this dilemma for 18 years in hopes of finding some solution, and a year after his death two treatises were published which set forth his answers.

In his *Disquisition on Government*, Calhoun makes a "great and broad distinction" between two types of government: constitutional and absolute. The test of a government is whether individuals and minority groups are protected in their interests against a monarch or majority by a constitution founded on compromise and long experience. If, however, a government should divide the citizens into two groups, those who pay the taxes and those who receive the benefits, then that government is a tyranny, no matter how egalitarian in theory. "And so," Kirk writes, "Calhoun comes to the doctrine of concurrent majorities, his most important single contribution to political thought."[44] A true majority, by Calhoun's understanding, is not a number of people told by a headcount; instead, it is a balancing and compromising of different interests, in which all the important aspects of the population are represented. Kirk quotes Calhoun,

> There are two different modes in which the sense of the community may be taken; one, simply by the right of suffrage, unaided; the other, by the right through a proper organism. Each collects the sense of the majority. But one regards numbers only, and considers the whole community as a unit, having but one common interest throughout; and collects the sense of the greater number of the whole, as that of the community. The other, on the contrary, regards interests as well as numbers—considering the community as made up of different and conflicting interests, as far as the action of the government is concerned; and takes the sense of each, through its majority or appropriate organ, and the united sense of all, as the sense of the entire community. The former of these I shall call the numerical, or absolute majority; and the latter, the concurrent, or constitutional majority.[45]

The great breakthrough Calhoun made with this new doctrine is the rejection of the abstraction called "the people." There is no such thing as a "people," existing as a homogeneous body of identical interests. In reality, there are only individuals and groups. Polling the numerical majority is unlikely to determine the sense of the true majority of interests and will probably result in granting all power to the urban concentrations of population, effectively disenfranchising the rural areas. For Calhoun, of course, the good Southerner that he was, this would never do. Votes ought to be weighed as well as counted, he thought, and not merely the individual votes of persons, but also the wills of the large groups of the nation, groups defined by their economic or geographical characteristics and protected from encroachment of one another by a check on the action of government. Calhoun believed common convenience would prevent such an arrangement from resulting in a perpetual stalemate, though even if such reorganization did slow the pace of government action, the gain in security from oppression would be worth it.

Calhoun further examined how such a government would affect liberty. Under the concurrent majority principle, he found that liberty would increase relative to the absolute majority system because each region or section of the populace would be free to shape its institutions and voice its political concerns as it wished; whereas in the current system, the majority tends to impose a standardized and arbitrary pattern on the whole of the nation. Complete equality, therefore, is incompatible with true liberty. Equality of condition would have to be enforced by an exercise of power to the detriment of liberty. If people in their groups and persons are left free to do as they choose, *inequality* is the natural outcome, as Calhoun tells us,

> Now, as individuals differ greatly from each other, in intelligence, sagacity, energy, perseverance, skill, habits of industry and economy, physical power, position and opportunity,—the necessary effect of leaving all free to exert themselves to better their condition, must be a corresponding inequality between those who may possess these qualities and advantages in a high degree, and those who may be deficient in them. The only means by which this result can be prevented are, either to impose such restrictions on the exertions of those who may possess them in a high degree, as will place them on a level with those who do not; or to deprive them of the fruits of their exertions. But to impose such restrictions on them would be destructive of liberty,—while, to deprive them of the fruits of their exertions, would be to destroy the desire of bettering their condition. It is, indeed, this inequality of condition between the front and rear ranks, in the march of progress, which gives so strong an impulse to the former to maintain their position, and to the latter to press forward into their files. This gives to progress its greatest impulse. To force the front rank back to the rear, or attempt to push forward the rear into line with the front, by the interposition of the government, would put an end to the impulse, and effectually arrest the march of progress.[46]

Calhoun's *Disquisition*, Kirk notes, is open to many common objections to detailed political projects, but certainly less so than the great reform schemes of our time, such as Marxism or production-planning. The point Kirk makes with Calhoun's ideas is that he described a philosophical principle, and one of most sagacious and vigorous ever advanced by American conservatism, at that. Kirk believes Calhoun's proposal merits him the title, along with John Adams, as one of the two most eminent American political writers. Calhoun, writes Kirk, "demonstrated that conservatism can project as well as complain."[47]

Kirk's last section of this chapter is a eulogy for the Southern conservatism of Randolph and Calhoun that was largely ignored by the antebellum South. Northern abolitionists and Southern fire-eaters descended into harangue and passion. Randolph and Calhoun left no disciples, and soon the industrial North smashed the agricultural South. Reconstruction finished the obliteration of the society of the Old South and subjugated it to the economic machine of modern times. "No political philosophy," Kirk notes, "has had a briefer span of triumph than that accorded Randolph's and Calhoun's."[48]

Chapter Six
Liberal Conservatives: Macaulay, Cooper, Tocqueville

In his sixth chapter, Kirk discusses men who deserve the name of conservative because they were, perhaps surprisingly to today's reader, liberal. Toward the end of the 19th century, British and American liberalism began to slide into collectivism, and has have since embraced it entirely. But there was a time when "liberals" loved "liberty," and so, prior to the middle of the century, political liberalism was a conservatism of a kind in that it tended to conserve liberty. Three liberals, Thomas Macaulay, J.F. Cooper, and Alexis de Tocqueville, foresaw the perils to personal freedom that lay on the horizon and so warrant attention in a study of the conservatism of this period.

Kirk notes that each of these men owes something to Burke, particularly Macaulay, whom Kirk calls an energetic eulogist, and whose works are rife with Burke's ideas. Personal and local freedoms, limited government, and intelligent reform, all dear to the liberal heart, are Burkean principles. Burke also taught them respect for private property and a suspicion of political power not built on the propertied interest. Macaulay was chosen, Kirk explains, to represent the conservative elements in British liberalism; Cooper is the most forthright thinker, among Americans, who stood for, in Kirk's words, "a democracy of elevation against a democracy of degradation;" and Tocqueville, of course, authored a most profound analysis of democracy.

Thomas Babington Macaulay, despite being included by Kirk, gets no light treatment. Kirk takes him to task for his inconsistent conservatism, particularly for his mistake in India, where, contrary to Burke, he recommended that the customs and traditions of India be submerged in a Westernization of the colony at British hands. He is also faulted for his failure to link social causes with social consequences. While Macaulay was uneasy with the swelling population of the industrial masses and their political power, he warmly praised industrialization, urbanization, and consolidation of every description. While he wrote glowing compliments for materialism, he was conscious of the danger presented by the possibility of the poor lower class receiving the vote. Macaulay wanted the efficient, progressive prosperity of industrial England to be kept safe from the proletariat. He endeavored therefore to push through the Reform Bill of 1866, which would permanently exclude from the franchise the unpropertied masses, an exclusion of the kind Burke had warned against. Macaulay's position was ultimately untenable, says Kirk, but he rendered to conservatism an honorable service in its defense.

Macaulay also deserves admiration for his sustained attack on Utilitarian principle. He ridiculed the Benthamites for their naive assumption that if the masses were enfranchised they would vote according to the best interests of the nation. Instead, Macaulay believed they would vote in their own, short-term self-interest, to rob the rich, regardless of the consequences. Kirk praises Macaulay by stating that he "brought into question every point of their logic and their view of human nature; he did them much harm; and because of that, he deserves the thanks of conservatives political and spiritual."[49] Macaulay understood the illiberal tendency of democracy, the danger of the poor plundering the rich, redistributing wealth according to some abstract notion of social justice, and he suggested two palliatives that might arrest the menace while preserving the form of government.

Education was one of the solutions Macaulay proposed, arguing, according to Kirk, that it just might be possible to persuade the poor man to revere his Maker, respect legitimate authority, and seek to redress wrongs by peaceful, constitutional means. Kirk wryly comments that this instruction is asking a great deal from schooling, and he fires a shot at Macaulay for his worry that ignorant violence might destroy "beautiful and costly machinery." Still, Kirk admits that Macaulay, in overestimating the power of state education, followed in the footsteps of Jefferson, Gladstone, and Disraeli, themselves in line with most men of the first half of the 19th century, failing to foresee the limitations of formal schooling.

Macaulay's second preventive was a rigid political constitution, one that would exclude the proletariat from the voting booth. But as Kirk has already noted, Macaulay was out of touch with reality. In any liberal government there will be pressure to level the economic playing field so long as a large portion of the population is poor. Kirk is rather heavy-handed in his dismissal, as follows:

> If one is to judge from the course of Western politics since Macaulay's day, this pressure is relieved only by the triumph of illiberal political systems or by some restoration of property, purpose, and dignity to the masses of a nation. Macaulay devised no provision for either course; he was neither a radical nor a true conservative; and so the Whigs from whom he descended are extinct, and the Liberals who succeeded him are moribund.[50]

Kirk devotes this chapter's third section to James Fenimore Cooper, a democrat of nineteenth-century America who was unflinching in his patriotism and unsparing in his criticism of American folly. He did his best, we read, to steer *a via media*, a middle way, between capitalistic consolidation and Southern separatism, and to reconcile the spirit of a gentleman with political equality. Cooper believed in freedom, progress, property, and gentility. For Kirk, he provides a link between the liberalism of Macaulay and the liberalism of Tocqueville.

Cooper's *The American Democrat* was his great contribution to political philosophy and the summation of his thought. Kirk calls it an endeavor to strengthen democracy by delineating its natural bounds. In it, Cooper undertakes to examine popular misconceptions that endanger private liberty, such as equality is not absolute, the Declaration of Independence is not to be literally understood, and the very existence of government implies inequality. It was his hope to awaken the people to the necessity for restraint in the exercise of their power; he also hoped in the survival of the gentleman, men who could lead their communities, men superior to vulgar impulses and intimidation. As Burke and Adams both knew, there are by nature some men better equipped to lead than others, and we ought to make it our concern to see that these natural aristocrats are endowed with a sense of civic duty and are stationed in the corridors of power. Cooper was concerned for the preservation of a gentleman landowner's right to his property, a right he saw dwindle before his own eyes. If democratic society robbed gentlemen of their means, how could it provide for its own leadership? Kirk warns that if the gentleman and the lady vanish from a society, eventually civilization will go with them. Cooper, he regrets, lost his fight for a democracy "studded with men of good birth and high principle."

> It is believed by some that modern society will be always changing its aspect; for myself, I fear that it will ultimately be too invariably fixed in the same institutions, the same prejudices, the same manners, so that mankind will be stopped and circumscribed; that the mind will swing backwards and forwards forever without begetting fresh ideas; that man will waste his strength in bootless and solitary trifling, and, though in continual motion, that humanity will cease to advance.[51]

With this quote from Tocqueville, Kirk begins this chapter's fourth section. Tocqueville, the only figure not British or American included in Kirk's work, authored a monumental examination of the spirit and tendency of American society and a classic of modern political theory, *Democracy in America*. While there is a wealth of wisdom to be found in it, Kirk limits himself to consideration of Tocqueville's "supreme achievement as a political theorist," the analysis of democratic despotism. Essentially, Tocqueville's concern was that in a democratic system mediocrity would become the standard, and would not only be encouraged, but enforced. Tocqueville's words demand their own hearing:

> Whenever social conditions are equal, public opinion presses with enormous weight upon the mind of each individual; it surrounds, directs, and

oppresses him; and this arises from the very constitution of society much more than from its political laws. As men grow more alike, each man feels himself weaker in regard to all the rest; as he discerns nothing by which he is considerably raised above them or distinguished from them, he mistrusts himself as soon as they assail him. Not only does he mistrust his strength, but he even doubts of his right, and he is very near acknowledging that he is in the wrong, when the great number of his countrymen assert that he is so. The majority do not need to force him; they convince him. In whatever way the powers of a democratic community may be organized and balanced, then, it will always be extremely difficult to believe what the bulk of the people reject or to profess what they condemn.[52]

What Tocqueville means by democratic despotism is that democracy will prey upon itself by dragging down the best men to the level of the mediocre, the average, the common man. What menaces democracy in this age is not anarchy or despotism by an individual, but the tyranny of mediocrity. Kirk believes Tocqueville foresaw the coming of the welfare state, the mother bureaucracy that seeks to provide everything for its children and exacts rigid conformity to that end. Again, Tocqueville, in his own words, describes such a state:

Above this race of men stands an immense and tutelary power, which takes upon itself alone to secure their gratifications and to watch over their fate. That power is absolute, minute, regular, provident, and mild. It would be like the authority of a parent if, like that authority, its object was to prepare men for manhood; but it seeks, on the contrary, to keep them in perpetual childhood; it is well content that the people should rejoice, provided that they think of nothing but rejoicing. For their happiness such a government willingly labors, but it chooses to be the sole agent and the only arbiter of their necessities, facilitates their pleasures, manages their principal concerns, directs their industry, regulates the descent of property, and subdivides their inheritances; what remains, but so spare them all the care of thinking and all the trouble of living?[53]

Democracy in America, Tocqueville goes on to note, has taken a bent toward materialism. If the middle class can convince the rest that material gratification is the object of life, none will rest until the government is reorganized to furnish them with what they desire. Such an impulse will tend to stifle creativity and freedom; it will weaken the higher faculties of man, and furthermore, it will be its own undoing. This absorption in getting and spending will undermine man's disposition to the infinite, to the spiritual, and so diminish his humanity. Such avarice also is harmful to the social structure that makes such a pursuit of wealth possible. As Kirk notes, moral decay will strangle honest government and regular commerce. There will be no more enjoyment in having, only in getting, and men will spurn involvement in society in favor of their selfish aggrandizement. People will cease governing themselves, and so, in Kirk's well-turned phrase, "compulsion is applied above as self-discipline relaxes below, and the last liberties expire under the weight of a unitary state."[54]

What ought conservatives to do about this dismaying picture of democracy's decline? How are we to fight the proclivity to uniformity, the willingness to place all real power in one central government, the hatred of hierarchy and degrees? Kirk informs us that Tocqueville believed men—and societies—possess free will. The historical forces which move the Western world toward democracy and its undesirable consequences are not inevitable. A determined stand, Kirk believes, could avert democratic despotism, a stand made by the force of ideas, the influence of the mind in service of the preservation of the old ways of society. Chief among these ideas for Kirk is religion, and here Tocqueville found some reassurance as well. Religion may help counteract the materialism that threatens to overwhelm; it may check the tendency to self-love so inimical to public service and inculcate the moral strength necessary for a people to govern themselves and so save their liberties.

Laws and customs, too, may keep a democracy from corruption, if they are established in the popular affections. In the United States, the federal framework of state powers, local government, and the independent judiciary, indeed decentralization in general, all keep from the majority the tools of tyranny; "so long as power can be denied to pure numbers, so long as great fields of human activity are exempt from the influence of government, so long as constitutions limit the scope of legislation—so long as these things endure, democratic despotism is kept at bay."[55]

Public education might also preserve a democratic society, provided it keeps Americans informed of their rights and duties. But above all, for Kirk, conservatives ought to nurture individual differences and variety of character. Real men should resist the power of the state should it attempt to mandate uniformity and mediocrity. Excellence, though it means inequality, can safeguard the nation from an overbearing collectivism by making it more difficult to standardize the people and rule them with a gloved but iron hand.

Tocqueville's legacy to conservatism, according to Kirk, is his strict and accurate criticism of its unfortunate weaknesses and his suggested reforms. His cause is not hopeless, says Kirk, for some men still resist conformity and will not rest silent while the mob takes the helm. "The people do not think or act uninfluenced by ideas and leaders. Without ideas and leaders, for that matter, a people cannot truly be said to exist. . . ."[56]

Chapter Seven
Transitional Conservatism: New England Sketches

Kirk begins his seventh chapter with a preface concerning the effects of the rise of industrialism and democracy on society. Because of these forces, "the physical and intellectual props of conservative order were knocked away."[57] Wealth changed hands, passing from the landed estates to the new industrial and financial enterprises in the cities. People began to move in large numbers from rural to urban areas. And, Kirk mourns, the new industrial man cared little for traditional values and ways of life. This new world was one "without veneration." While the social order underwent upheaval, so, too, did the intellectual realm, and Kirk indicts rationalism and utilitarianism for undermining the foundations of the old system. Conservatives were no longer as sure of themselves in the face of the rationalist onslaught from Jacobin France and the Benthamites. "Conservatism had become uncertain how to reply to sophisters and calculators; the poetic vehemence of the Romantics had deserted them, and they had not yet acquired the methods of the legal and historical conservatives who appeared in Victorian times."[58] Still, New England could lay claim to a few "men of genius," men of conservative stripe who did what they could in the decades preceding the War Between the States to divert the flow of change into the channels of tradition.

This chapter's second section examines the contributions of John Quincy Adams, a conservative of talent who unfortunately, says Kirk, distrusted the ideals he was supposed to champion. In fact, Kirk's assessment of Adams' efficacy as a leader and a thinker is, at best, a mixed bag. He lauds Adams' candor, his diligence, and his noble intentions, but he seems to believe that ultimately Adams was insufficient for the task at hand. His public life soured him and unsettled his views of God and man; he began as a conservative and ended as an abolitionist, helping to fan the flames that would eventually consume the nation. His conservatism was mitigated by certain radical tendencies, among them his belief in the perfectibility of man, his enthusiasm for the consolidation of power for human betterment, and his excessive praise for democracy.

Adams wanted to use the power of the federal government to encourage manufacturing, promote science, befriend liberty around the world, improve the nation's infrastructure, and conserve the public lands of the West. Strange that today such goals seem commonplace—a measure, perhaps, of how far supposed "conservatives" have drifted. He thought he was fulfilling Washington's idea of union in pushing for roads, canals, tariffs, and industries at federal expense. He wanted to lift the nation to a higher plane of social progress, to fashion a republic free and benevolent, full of hope and prosperity. His was a lofty idea. "It was quite impossible."[59]

Adams did not realize the depth of American resistance to direction from above, explains Kirk; he forgot with whom he was dealing. His mistake makes his defeat in the race for a second presidential term against Andrew Jackson less than a surprise. Jackson proposed to give the people what they wanted, and he got twice as many electoral votes as a result. Adams, Kirk implies, believed God had abandoned him, and he never really recovered from his defeat. When he was elected to the House of Representatives, he began to exact revenge against the South, his perceived enemy. Kirk does not believe Adams' detestation of slavery only came about after his defeat but sees in Adams' constant presentation of abolitionist petitions a fruit at least nourished by his bitterness toward "Jackson's South."[60] Kirk of course recognizes that Adams was right to hate the peculiar institution but admonishes us that "in clothing himself with the braver of a reformer, Adams forgot the prudence of a conservative.[61] He allowed himself to be warmed by the climate of opinion into a flirtation with a dangerous, radical movement, and after him, "the deluge."[62]

In section three, Kirk examines a man who could scarcely be imagined a conservative: Ralph Waldo Emerson. Among several literary figures who lent their talents to the advancement of the same doctrines Adams had espoused—infinite material progress, perfectibility, and alteration for its own sake—Emerson's name was pre-eminent. Kirk is convinced that Emerson's ideas resonated with popular American sentiment at the time, ideas such as reliance on personal emotion and private judgment, contempt for prescription and the experience of the species, and an egocentric social morality. Kirk denigrates Emerson's style but admits that "[his] speculations were so congenial to the American temper that their influence upon American thought has been incalculably great. . . ."[63]

For all his disturbing spiritual individualism, however, Kirk takes greatest issue with Emerson's politics. "Emerson's specific political notions are almost shocking—frightening in the first instance for their perilous naivete, in the second instance for their easy indifference to uncomfortable facts."[64] Emerson was confident that all that is necessary to government is good will. Political systems will do just fine, so long as they are founded on "absolute right," to be established by the violent hero, the "wise man" reformer. (Emerson believed John Brown, of Harper's Ferry fame, was the destined instrument of absolute right.) Emerson's greatest fault, however, was his failure to acknowledge the reality of sin, a cardinal tenet of conservatism. Emerson simply dismisses this idea, and as a result, "the whole social tendency of Emersonianism has been either to advocate some radical and summary measure, a Solomon's judgment without its saving cunning, or (if this will not suffice) to pretend that the problem does not exist."[65] Emerson, it is clear, was a radical, perhaps the most influential radical in America, ready to discard the old social order for a sentimental dream.

In section four Kirk turns to the obscure author Orestes Brownson, a Vermont Roman Catholic who exemplifies, at least for Kirk, the progress of that religion as a conservative force in America. Brownson was no friend to Protestantism. In fact, he believed it wholly inadequate to the task of sustaining popular liberty, for, as he saw it, Protestant faith was itself subject to popular will, passion, or caprice. It lacked authority, so the argument goes, to preserve Christianity from degenerating into a plethora of "fanatic sects and egotistical professions." Kirk, a Romanist himself, fervently agreed in his assessment of Brownson's critique. To Brownson, Protestantism is an expression of the modern spirit and so is hostile to submission to government. Brownson fulminates, "What [the modern spirit] hates is not this or that form of government, but *legitimacy*, and it would rebel against democracy as quick as against absolute monarchy, if democracy were asserted on the ground of legitimacy."[66] Such a rebellious spirit is damning for democracy, stimulating disorder and breaking apart the moral stability necessary for a people to govern themselves. With this weakness, Protestantism cannot provide the moral authority needed to check human appetite. Kirk notes, "As Protestantism and its fumbling offshoots decay before our eyes, upon the mound of dissent must rise the fortress of orthodox belief, without which human sin and foible know no limits, without which order and justice perish."[67]

Brownson, in his *The American Republic*, expressed his concerns over the American urge to fashion everything out of whole cloth. He was sure that no reform or change in our society or government will be successful unless it has roots in the past, because man does not create—he continues and develops. Providence is continuing creation; denying Providence is to condemn ourselves to restless stagnation. It is Kirk's hope that the Catholicism in America will resurrect such intelligence as Brownson's and reconcile orthodoxy with Americanism.

In the fifth section Kirk discusses the contributions of Nathaniel Hawthorne, whom he considers the most influential conservative New England thinker of this period. Hawthorne restored to the American mind the doctrine of sin Emerson neglected. Kirk finds that his influence on American thought is twofold. His other contribution, the perpetuation of the past, is addressed first.

"Conservatism," Kirk declares, "cannot exist anywhere without reverence for dead generations."[68] In like manner to Scott and other authors like Irving and Cooper, Hawthorne created a vision of an American story to remind the national imagination of our heritage. He leavened the American temper, as Kirk puts it, with a respect for old things—in Hawthorne's case, the old things of Puritan New England, his especial province. Through such works as *The Scarlet Letter, The House of Seven Gables, Twice Told Tales,* and *Mosses from an Old Manse*, Hawthorne showed the Puritan spirit for what it was, severe in its morality, suspicious of alteration, and contemptuous of materialism. Such a spirit, Kirk knows, is abhorrent to the modern American mindset, but because of Hawthorne, we shall never be able to forget the Puritans.

This achievement of Hawthorne's is secondary, however, to his preoccupation with the idea of sin, which Kirk calls his obsession, his vocation, and almost his life. Hawthorne stood firmly in his denouncement of iniquity, becoming a "major preceptor" of conservatives, as he taught with his literary mastery that the only reform really worth the bother is reform of conscience. Not that Hawthorne made the doctrine of sin popular, but he did make a great number of people aware of it. This, says Kirk, is his powerful conservative achievement. Hawthorne flatly contradicted Emerson, describing in his works the consequence of sin-blind humanitarian endeavor: catastrophe. "A lurking consciousness of sin has haunted American letters ever since."[69]

Kirk goes on to describe four works of Hawthorne's, *The Blithedale Romance, The Hall of Fantasy, The Celestial Railroad,* and *Earth's Holocaust.* Space does not permit exploration of these excellent stories; in short, each of them demonstrates Hawthorne's conviction that moral reformation is the only real reformation, that sin left out of the humanitarian equation will come back to haunt—literally, in Hawthorne's case—any such effort.

Chapter Eight
Conservatism With Imagination: Disraeli and Newman

Kirk's eighth chapter examines one famous radical and two more obscure conservative figures of 19th century England. Karl Marx is examined in the first section and provides a contrasting background to the conservatives discussed later. Marx and Engels issued *The Communist Manifesto* in 1848 and *Das Capital* in 1867. Despite Marx's materialistic currents, Kirk notes that Marx's idealism and concerns with end-states captured the imaginations of contemporary English Liberals, who were much more concerned with the means to those ends.

Marx's great end of human behavior, Kirk tells us, is absolute equality of condition. He had no illusions of natural equality; he intended to make it. By legislation and economic device the socialist must create equality for all men. In Kirk's words: "The clever, the strong, the industrious, the virtuous, must be compelled to serve the weak and stupid and slack and vicious; nature must submit to the socialist art."[70] Still, Kirk says, as arbitrary as this mythical Equality is, it has more imagination in it than the Utilitarian idea of "the greatest happiness for the greatest number." So, says Kirk, as the radical impulse left Bentham for Marx, Envy triumphed over Self-Interest.

The imagination and ends of the conservatives in this chapter were of another nature. Their idea was Order, and they, as statesmen and philosophers, contended as Tory reformers to restore what had been lost to industrialism and the corrosive Benthamite philosophy.

The second section of this chapter examines the life and work of the conservative Jewish statesman, Benjamin Disraeli. Like Marx, Disraeli's idea of a proper British society involved classes. Unlike Marx, however, he believed classes to be good and necessary for the state, and his aim in politics was to reconcile the classes into one nation. In his words, "Class is order; without order, law crumbles."[71] The Tory, Kirk states, must seek to infuse into modern industrial life the aristocratic spirit, the loyalty to persons and places, and the rudiment of conservatism. To Disraeli, the British constitution had suffered through the Reformation, the Revolution, the Restoration, the Glorious Revolution, and the French Revolution, and it was his task to set about restoring national tradition and character, recognizing that all classes had a right to be heard. In *A Vindication of the English Constitution, The Letters of Runnymede, Coningsby,* and *Sybil*, Kirk tells us, these ideas were set forth.

After the Reform Bill disaster of 1832, the Tories under the leadership of Sir Robert Peel had languished; not until the Corn Law question was Peel repudiated and the party reconstituted under Disraeli and Derby. After 1873, the Conservatives (the Tories) gained and kept office for most of the next three decades. But Disraeli's chief achievement, Kirk asserts, was implanting in the public imagination an *ideal* of Toryism that was valuable in keeping Britain faithful to her constitution. Nowhere else in the modern world has a unified conservative party enjoyed such continuity of purpose and popular support (Kirk passed away in 1994; the rise of the Labour party to continued power was unknown to him), a success for which Disraeli is responsible.

It was no small task that confronted the British statesman. The working classes of his native land had sunk to a low and miserable condition. "Lodged in the most miserable tenements in the most hideous burgh in the ugliest country in the world," the poor industrial laborers were also ignorant of religion, believing in "our Lord and Saviour Pontius Pilate who was crucified to save our sins; and in Moses, Goliath, and the rest of the Apostles."[72] (These are the Disraeli's words, not Kirk's.) But Disraeli was undaunted; he knew there was still much worth saving in Britain. As he put it,

> You have an ancient, powerful, richly-endowed Church, and perfect religious liberty. You have unbroken order and complete freedom. You have landed estates as large as the Romans', combined with commercial enterprise such as Carthage and Venice united never equaled. And you must remember that this peculiar country, with these strong contrasts, is not governed by force; it is not governed by standing armies; it is governed by a most singular series of traditionary influences, which generation after generation cherishes because it knows that they are out of all proportion to the essential and indigenous elements and resources of the country. If you destroy that state of society, remember this—England cannot begin again.[73]

To remedy his ailing country, Disraeli proposed reviving national identity and restoring true religious feeling. He also saw a need for a series of political and economic amendments to reinvigorate the Church, renew reverence for the Crown, preserve local governments, recognize the agricultural interest, and improve the physical condition of the working classes. And all this was to be restoration, not revolution. To Kirk, Disraeli's guidance helped the Conservatives succeed in much of their program, for today, Great Britain is the only great power on earth that experienced no revolution or civil war during either the 19th or 20th centuries. This, Kirk proclaims, is a magnificent conservative achievement.

The second philosopher-conservative discussed in this chapter is John Henry

Newman. A reluctant controversialist, Newman fought back against what he perceived to be the weakening of the Church of England by Utilitarian encroachments. He was the leader of the Oxford Movement, which, with aid from Evangelicals and even some dissenters, was able to abate the assault, though the Church has never been the same.

For Newman, true knowledge resulted in man acting upon it. Physical science does not bring conviction, for the most plausible scientific theories are based on mere suppositions from facts assembled in our faulty human way. Secular knowledge is not a principle of moral improvement, nor a means of it, nor the antecedent to it. In fact, Newman thought that secular knowledge without personal religion is often a tool of unbelief. True knowledge is not the product of orderly reason or Benthamite logic, not the result of instruction in physical and moral science. Instead, knowledge is really the fruit of what Newman called the Illative Sense. By this men comprehend first principles, those things without which all the practical knowledge in the world is but a goad to torment man, a burden to bore him. "Life is for action," Newman declares; "If we insist on proofs for everything, we shall never come to action: to act you must assume, and that assumption is faith."[74] The true source of our first principles, of our motives for living, the power of judging and concluding, is the Illative Sense. Kirk describes it as "the combined product of intuition, instinct, imagination, and long and intricate experience."[75] Of course, no man's Illative Sense is infallible; it must be corrected by reference to authority, which could mean conscience, the Church, antiquity, or the Bible. Newman believed physical science could not tell us much about history or ethics, for in those fields we have not got facts. Such studies must be undertaken by the Illative Sense, the ultimate sanction of belief and action. The Utilitarians, who studiously ignored Faith as nonscientific, undercut their own system, for on their own terms, religion is a strong prop of society, a deterrent to evil, and a consolation to man. Only by this Sense can a man ever climb out of doubt, says Kirk; only by it can a man rouse himself to live, to act. First principles rule the world, because they rule the hearts of men. So much cannot be said for the scientific method.

Perhaps even more significant for conservatism are Newman's thoughts on liberal education, for which he was an ardent advocate. It was Newman's contention that the problem for statesmen of his day was how to educate the masses, who were generally newcomers to political power. Education, for Newman, was a discipline of the mind, not the accumulation of inert facts or the learning of a craft. While education cannot teach virtue, the discipline that accompanies education is like virtue, and the root of education in any case is theology. In his famous *The Idea of a University* Newman first proves that theology is a science before considering the general question of what higher education ought to be. A Tory, Newman never dealt with the problem he set for statesmen; he turned his attention to preparing society's leading elements, its gentlemen. By liberal education Newman means "a habit of mind is formed which lasts through life, of which the attributes are, freedom, equitableness, calmness, moderation, and wisdom; or what in a former discourse I have ventured to call the philosophical habit."[76] This is the education of a free man, knowledge pursued for its own sake, discipline achieved for the good of the mind. It cannot instill virtue, true, but it teaches right reason and brings order to the active intellect. Newman's own words are best,

> This process of training, by which the intellect, instead of being formed or sacrificed to some particular or accidental purpose, some specific trade or profession, or study or science, is disciplined for its own sake, for the perception of its own proper object, and for its own highest culture, is called Liberal Education; and though there is no one in whom it is carried as far as is conceivable, or whose intellect would be a pattern of what intellects should be made, yet there is scarcely any one but may gain an idea of what real training is, and at least look towards it, and make its true scope and result, not something else, his standard of excellence.[77]

Thus it is not learning or acquirement but reason exercised upon knowledge that is the end of education for Kirk and Newman.

We have fallen far from such an ideal of education. Britain began down this path by the mid-19th century and has not looked back. The Liberals pressed for the need for technical training to stay competitive with Germany and insure industrial prosperity. The Benthamite model of secular, uniform, and compulsory education slowly took shape; today it dominates Britain and America. Nevertheless, as Kirk notes, a conservative thinker ought to be judged on what he preserves, not what he fails to avert. On that score, Newman did very well. He has kept in the minds of many professors and educated men an ideal of education that continues to struggle against the decline of learning into training for widget-making. Kirk concludes: "that grim utilitarian expediency continues to be opposed by the ancient religious view of society—this is Newman's bequest, in greater part than some historians of ideas acknowledge, to the England whose spiritual and literary tradition he loved and enriched."[78]

Chapter Nine
Legal and Historical Conservatism: A Time of Foreboding

Conservatism in England in the last three decades of the 19th century underwent changes that brought the Tory party closer to the positions of their old adversaries, the Liberals. What had happened? Socialism happened. The policies of the Liberals, particularly their enfranchising of the working class, led to an expanding state and an aggressive labor movement. In response, the middle classes threw their support to the Tories, who saw that the danger lay in a greedy democracy and a ponderous government. Collectivism, with John Stuart Mill's secular materialism as forerunner, was threatening the liberties secured by the British constitution, and so the Tory party became the champion of individualism against "all manner of socialists." Kirk points to three champions of the embattled conservatism of this era: James Fitzjames Stephen, Henry Maine, and W.E.H. Lecky.

Stephen began life as strict Utilitarian, and his teachers, whom he never repudiated, were Hobbes, Locke, Bentham, and John Austin. It was a grave error of theirs which made a conservative out of the man: they ignored the depravity of man. This chapter's second section covers Stephen, who is perhaps best known for his work, *Liberty, Equality, Fraternity* (1873), with which he launched a broadside at his nemesis, J.S. Mill. While the book had little influence in his time, Stephen's essay is still the best reply to Mill's doctrines besides being written as a refutation of the principles of the French Republic. Kirk identifies two points that made a conservative out of the Utilitarian Stephen: his concept of the state and his opinion of human nature.

Like his father, the younger Stephen believed that everything in society is derived from religious truth. Anyone pursuing abstract notions of liberty, equality, and fraternity, devoid of religious reverence, is slouching toward servitude. Indeed, the state was created to enforce law based on principles derived from religion. Of course, the need for any sort of government, leads us to the second and more significant of Stephen's conservative convictions, original sin. Stephen knew that man is evil by nature and can only overcome his more base appetites by divine aid; he knew it well enough, in fact, that Kirk calls this belief the foundation of Stephen's politics. Stephen wrote of Mill that he believed men would live as brothers if emancipated and made equal. On the contrary, Stephen believed "[that] many men are bad, a vast majority of men indifferent, and many good, and that the great mass of indifferent people sway this way or that according to circumstances. . . ."[79] He scoffed at the whole idea of equality. Men would never achieve moral parity, and it was therefore obvious that the good and wise ought to rule the bad. Indifferent to God or an afterlife, the state and the morality it enforces will collapse. But, by recognizing God, the state can help lead men to their proper end, which, Stephen insists, is not happiness, but virtue. By being righteous, men can know the greatest happiness possible, rather than by Utilitarian legislation designed to increase their material comfort. But whatever system men adhere to, Stephen believed, the religion of the French Revolution is deadly; "whichever rule is applied, there are vast numbers of matters in respect of which men ought not to be free; they are fundamentally unequal, and they are not brothers at all, or only under qualifications which make the assumption of their fraternity unimportant."[80]

Thus, Stephen demonstrated that the philosophical assumptions of the Jacobins and Mill alike were rotten to the core. But, as Kirk explains, even if these glaring errors are left aside, Mill's position is still untenable, for he is guilty of a fundamental, internal mistake, which is that he believed society could be ruled by discussion. Stephen knew societies were ruled by force. His definition of force comprehended more than physical compulsion, however; the fear of Hell, public opinion, and even discussion itself is a veil for force of a kind. Society can appear to be ruled by opinion or discussion, but only if the opposing interests are evenly balanced. Otherwise, groups of men will make it quite clear that they are ready to resort to physical violence to make their case. Kirk mentions mobs at Nottingham and Bristol prior to the Reform of 1832 as evidence. Man can always be improved by discussion, Stephen allows, but force is the indispensable prop to order: "to say that the law of force is abandoned because force is regular, unopposed, and beneficially exercised, is to say that night and day are now such well-founded institutions that the sun and moon are superfluities."[81] Modern states have at their disposal better-trained and equipped forces than ever before; so is order kept.

In his third section Kirk takes a look at Sir Henry Maine, who, like Burke, began his political life as a moderate Liberal, hoping to promote cautious reform and reconcile old and new interests. He made his mark on conservatism with the very study that made him conservative—his study of social history, a study that convinced him the drift of Western society was retrogressive, toward socialism. The founder of modern comparative social studies, Maine knew that human progress is a fragile creation, the achievement of high intellectual attainment and liberty under law coming only after centuries of effort. He measured progress by the index of the movement from status to contract, the principal instruments of that progress being private property and freedom of contract.

Maine was not dismal in his prospects for man, says Kirk. His study of the history of institutions showed that, with prudence and wisdom, man may progress. Though most of the time mankind tends to stagnate, there is a path to improvement. The Greeks found it, and so can we, if we follow proper scientific methods. The severe flaws of the

Benthamite theory of human nature might be corrected by the study of customs and inherited ideas it tosses aside as insignificant. Maine found that in primitive stages of society, men live in a condition of status; individuality was very rudimentary, property was held by groups, and life in general was dependent on the community. Progress, for Maine, is release from this condition. Civilized people move to a condition of contract, of several (private) property and individual achievement. Kirk quotes Maine, as follows:

> The movement of the progressive societies has been uniform in one respect. Through all its course it has been distinguished by the gradual dissolution of family dependency, and the growth of individual obligation in its place. The Individual is steadily substituted for the Family, as the unit of which civil laws take account...Nor is it difficult to see what is the tie between man and man which replaces by degrees those forms of reciprocity in rights and duties which have their origin in the Family. It is Contract. Starting, as from one terminus of history, from a condition of society in which all the relations of Persons are summed up in the relations of Family, we seem to have steadily moved towards a phase of social order in which all these relations arise from the free agreement of individuals.[82]

Besides allowing for more wealth and leisure, Maine believed contract society also provided a better form of moral education, because it taught the necessity of fidelity. Kirk thinks this brings Maine's Liberalism beyond the Utilitarians and up to that of Burke.

Maine also wrote *Popular Government*, in which he applied the historical judgments of his scholarship to the trends of government in Western society. It was Maine's contention that popular government was born with a lie in the cradle—the state of nature, which he dismisses as non-historical and unverifiable. By that fiction, however, democracy is held to be innately superior to any other form of government, regardless of failure. Maine was not convinced. To him, history proved that democracy possessed some serious flaws, among them an ultra-conservatism of thought and a taste for flattery, which means bribery. There were remedies for democratic imperfections, however; Maine thought that a suitably humble democracy, modest in its functions, combined with an exact and august constitution, could rescue popular government from itself; "It would seem that, by a wise Constitution, Democracy may be made nearly as calm as water in a great artificial reservoir; but if there is a weak point anywhere in the structure, the mighty force which it controls will burst through it and spread destruction far and near."[83]

In the fourth section, Kirk examines the contributions of W.E.H. Lecky, whose *Democracy and Liberty* he calls the most thorough manual of conservative politics of the

19th century. Its theme is abhorrence of radical change. Written against the background of secularizing education, increasing taxation of the propertied classes by the poor, and centralizing government, Lecky bemoaned in his work the robbing of the propertied classes, violating their rights and destroying the pattern of rural British life. Kirk calls Lecky the best spokesman of the landed and upper-middle classes in late-Victorian England. He opposed destroying the balance of interests in the community, opposed a democracy that would fall in love with regulation, and oppposed restrictions on property rights and other old freedoms.

Even worse, the direction of English Radicalism, according to Kirk, is currently toward socialism, which Lecky called slavery. The democracy is voting itself benefits at the expense of its wealthier members, granting more and more power to the central government to regulate and plan the economy. But neither Lecky nor Kirk is convinced socialism can actually survive in Britain. By all appearances, the 1980s seem to have proven them right, and the 1990s have perhaps proven them wrong. Britain is still in the grip of the Labour party and its overbearing collectivism. The House of Lords has all but been abolished. Perhaps what is needed is another reconciliation of the inheritors of Burke's liberal ideas, as Kirk puts it, with the conservatives of today's England, for the purpose of navigating the ship of state back to its proper course.

Chapter Ten
Conservatism Frustrated: America, 1865-1918

The America of Reconstruction and the Gilded Age was not the best time for conservatives, to say the least. It was a "half-century of frustration;" the South was in the throes of a protracted and agonizing recovery from the War Between the States, and the North was not prepared to take the leadership role it should have to restore a conservative order to a broken nation. What conservative thought there was to be found in this dark era was more in the line of English Liberalism, Kirk informs us, and was represented by James Russell Lowell, E.L. Godkin, Henry Adams, and Brooks Adams. Kirk gives a sad depiction of the challenges that lay ahead of these men of conservative principle, writing,

> The state of the nation was dismaying. This was the age of the exploiting financiers, the invincible city bosses with Tweed their *primus inter pares,* and the whole rout of grasping opportunists who are the reverse side of the coin of American individualism. Bryce's calm chapters in *The American Commonwealth* tell the story. This was the age, too, of a relentless economic centralization, a dull standardization, and an insatiable devastation of natural resources. Presently an abused public begins to stir in heavy resentment, and then in active protest; and that public resolves to cure the ills of democracy by introducing a greater degree of democracy. If democracy is corrupt—why, make it wholly popular: and so the last third of the 19th century experiences the successful advocacy of direct democratic devices. . . .Such democracy, however direct in name, is a sham: real power is captured...by special interests and clever organizers and the lobbies. A long way removed, this, from New England visions of the American future.[84]

James Russell Lowell is discussed in section two. Kirk writes of him as having little original genius but a generous amount of high talent, nonetheless. He founded the major American school of literary criticism and was an able poet, though early on his poetry was of a radical variety. Kirk regrets that Lowell never found his way out of a bitter antipathy for all things Southern. Lowell was an abolitionist and a virulent detractor of Jefferson Davis; as Kirk points out, such blind detestation from a man who should have known better did not sit well on a pupil of Burke.

Nevertheless, Lowell was a natural defender of tradition, hailing from "Brahmin New England" and calling himself a natural Tory. He was a Republican, and while he never called himself a Radical, he was allied with that wing of the party until President Johnson's impeachment, when he recognized the depths of vanity and spite to which the Republicans were descending. After this turning point in his life, he spent the rest of it working alongside the reform element of the party. He was disturbed, says Kirk, by the dissolution of manners, the loss of morals, the mass-mind of the uneducated and the deluge of immigrants, and while his solutions were vague and inconsistent, his insights sometimes "glow with conservative acuity and prudence."[85]

"After the Civil War, Lowell's chief contribution to politics was his endeavor to preserve the remnants of a gentlemanly tradition in defiance of the Gilded Age."[86] But what were his proposed solutions and the means he expected to use to arrive at them? Kirk asks these questions and finds the answers wanting. Lowell offered two propositions: education and amelioration of large inequalities of condition and fortune. Education is a fine thing, but how would education discipline the desires of a populace new to power? How would it prepare future leaders to exercise wisdom and restraint when the citizens forget? And how would those "enormous inequalities" be corrected? Lowell despised labor unions, wage legislation and state socialism in general, but he had small ability as a practical statesman, in Kirk's estimation, and his defect limited the value of his proposals. Whatever his lack of skill, however, he fought valiantly for a conservative republic, and with eloquence; in this troubled time, that is enough to deserve remembrance.

Section three describes the work Edwin Lawrence Godkin, the brilliant editor of *Nation* and an immigrant from Great Britain. Kirk identifies him as a Whig in the line of Macaulay and a shrewd critic who hoped to use his abilities to produce a "grave, decorous, and mature" press like England's to counteract the frivolity of the American newspaper industry. While Godkin was a sober conservative voice in the midst of the fray, during his tenure as editor of *Nation* his attempt to turn the papers failed.

Kirk thinks Godkin's most penetrating contribution to the analysis of modern society is his essay, "The Growth and Expression of Public Opinion," reprinted in *Unforeseen Tendencies of Democracy*. Firm in his belief that democracy was here to stay, Godkin's concern was that popular government would sink into a general mediocrity of mind and character. Particularly, Godkin worried that the people will not supply a government of good and qualified men. The public is bored with politics most of the time, allowing manipulators, criminals, and showmen to grasp power, though they might "swing the pendulum" and deny any party extended control of the helm. Democracies, he feared, tended to disregard or dislike men of special fitness; natural leaders were shut out by the envy of the multitude, leaving a vacuum that the cunning were happy to fill. This lack of competency and integrity in government is made worse by the modern state being shorn of the veneration and consecration Burke so loved. Godkin laments the loss, as follows:

"The state has lost completely, in the eyes of the multitude, the moral and intellectual authority it once possessed. It does not any longer represent God on earth. In democratic countries it represents the party which secured most votes at the last election, and is, in many cases, administered by men whom no one would make guardians of his children or trustees of his property. When I read the accounts given by the young lions of the historical school of the glorious future which awaits us as soon as we get the proper amount of state interference with our private concerns for the benefit of the masses, and remember that in New York, 'the state' consists of the Albany Legislature under the guidance of Governor Hill, and in New York City of the little Tammany junta known as 'the Big Four,' I confess I am lost in amazement."[87]

Still, as Kirk notes, even such a government might not wreck society, if the state could be limited by strict bounds. No such luck, however; modern populations, persuaded by mass media that they know whereof they vote, demand the extension of government beyond its old functions of external defense and internal order. The public is fascinated, in Kirk's words, at the possibility of getting necessities and comforts through the action of the state. Government manipulates the money supply and taxes one class to provide largesse for another. Compulsory education is undertaken at enormous public expense, roads are built, banks are founded, land is bought, and on and on it goes, making a Sherwood Forest of the nation's capital.

What are Godkin's prescriptions for these ailments? He does provide some practical remedies, and Kirk thinks that Godkin occasionally saw they all depended on the moral condition of the public capable of checking modern desires. Kirk lists the proposals: civil-service reform, the referendum, the initiative, the frequent constitutional convention, and governmental failure in managing the economy leading to *laissez-faire* policies' restoration. Unfortunately, these attempts to fix democracy with more democracy have failed miserably. The American people have thankfully avoided the extreme medicine of a constitutional convention, but they have only grumbled as the federal government steals more and more power. Money is now only worth what the government promises it is, or, more accurately, what the rest of the world thinks the government's promise is worth. Kirk views Godkin's limitations as those of any 19th-century liberal—the expectation that the masses would be reasonable with power. This does not make Godkin a failure, and Kirk gives him credit for his endeavor to turn the instruments of public opinion to good use. But he qualifies his praise by commenting that Godkin status as the most respectable opponent of innovation in the Gilded Age is evidence of the "dismal fatigue" of the era's conservatism.

The man discussed in section four was brilliant, witty, mocking, pessimistic, and highly educated. On the one hand, Kirk names Henry Adams the most irritating man in American letters. On the other, Adams is said to be the best historian this country ever produced. He was possessed of an exhaustive knowledge of medieval Europe and was thoroughly familiar with Japan, in addition having insights into the effects of science on culture. But his outlook of conservatism, in Kirk's words, was grim: "[His view of conservatism was] the view of a man who sees before him a steep and terrible declivity, from which there can be no returning. . . ."[88] Adams gained his bitterness through years of experience and learning. He taught history at Harvard for a few years and edited *The North American Review*, though his desire was to become a political leader through the law and the press. Defeated in both goals, he retreated to France and his study of the 13th century; in the Gilded Age, Adams could not serve in politics with success or honor.

Adams was disgusted by the rampant corruption of modern life, a sickness he detected in Britain, the Continent, and even young America, and he spent half his life investigating the sources of the disease. He rejected the popular answers to his question, Kirk says, in favor of an understanding of a "tremendous and impersonal process of degradation,"[89] a process involving the forces of science and history that would roll over all opposition until civilization would rot from the weight of socialism. Adams was convinced that the real struggle was not between men but between the forces driving the men. Society had been steadily lusting after centralization and physical power, and had now begun the final turn from what he called the Virgin, representative of spiritual power, to the Dynamo, physical power. Men were giving up religion and veneration for science. The old free community for which the illustrious Adamses had fought was being replaced by a unified state, one tending toward socialism because it is cheaper than capitalism, "and modern life always rewards cheapness."[90] Society was being driven like a machine toward its own moral and physical destruction, attracted by the promises of technological advancement science had made.

Adams' arguments found condensed expression in his *The Degradation of the Democratic Dogma*, in which three essays, *The Tendency of History, The Rule of Phase Applied to History,* and *A Letter to American Teachers of History*, put forth his supporting evidence. Kirk gives a brief summary of Adams' main point, writing, as in nature the exhaustion of energy is an inevitable reality, so also all social energies must give out in the end. The laws of thermodynamics doom us; all things tend toward disorder, including civilization, and so while nothing is added or subtracted to the sum of energy, intensity is always lost, and the energy dissipates like water doing work only by running downhill. Adams believed human activity had reached its greatest intensity in the Middle Ages with the building of the great cathedrals and the Crusades, and since then our vitality has been rapidly waning. "Industrialized," Kirk intones, "we are that much nearer to social ruin and total extirpation. 'The dead alone give us energy,' says Le Bon, and we moderns, having severed our ties with the past, are not long for this world."[91]

Adams might have had an antidote for his bleak forecast in Christian faith, but Kirk reports that he could not make himself believe in Providence. He believed history had to be "scientific," by which he meant it had to follow the theories of such men as Kelvin and Thomson. He might revere the Virgin, but he could not really worship a God. Kirk chronicles the decline of faith in the Adams family, and a sad story it is.

> The blunt nonconformist piety of John Adams gave way to the doubts of John Quincy Adams, the humanitarianism of Charles Francis Adams, the despair of Henry Adams. Belief in Providence, so enduringly rooted in Burke's conservatism, was lost in the vicissitudes of New England's conservative thought.[92]

Here Henry Adams' conservatism breaks down, for if the sanctions of religion are removed, the very basis for the dignity of man and the morality proper to him, what is left to conserve? Kirk leaves the question unanswered, and turns instead to Brooks Adams, who like his brother was fascinated by the determinism whose consequences he hated.

Section five examines the political culmination of the ideas of the house of Adams. Brooks Adams' credentials, however, are cast into doubt from the very beginning. After less than a paragraph, Kirk notes that Brooks' conservatism is "debatable." Disgusted with American society, Brooks thought the only hope for survival was the acceptance of progress and change. He denounced the capitalists and bankers loudly enough to make Marx proud, yet Kirk says he detested the very process he urged society to accept, longing for the republic of John Adams' day and condemning democracy as the cause and symptom of social decay. The general theme of his four books, *The Laws of Civilization and Decay, America's Economic Supremacy, The New Empire,* and *The Theory of Social Revolutions*, is his cyclical theory of history and his belief that man is captive to economic force. (This idea was reminiscent of his brother's.) Civilization, he maintained, is the product of centralization. Men come together and concentrate their political and economic power in cities before going out to conquer the simpler rural classes. From the Romans to the New World, men have made society wealthier by centralization, expansion, and subjugation, until the process reaches its highest point and the beginning of its end: the usurer. The money-lender, the economic man, saps social vitality and undermines the great centralized economy that produced him until barbarism regains mastery, and then the whole cycle begins anew. The usurer is the harbinger of the end, for in him all has been sacrificed to the money-making impulse, and he represents the society that made him; "Too stupid even to glimpse the necessity for revering and obeying the law that shelters him from social revolution, the capitalist lacks capacity sufficient for the administration of the society he has made his own."[93]

For all his antipathy for capitalism, centralization, and socialism, Brooks Adams still accepted consolidation as inevitable. For him, conservatism was doomed to die by the impersonal forces of economic destiny. Such a love for tradition, Adams wrote, "resists change instinctively and not intelligently, and it is this conservatism which largely causes those violent explosions of pent-up energy which we term revolutions....With conservative populations slaughter is nature's remedy."[94] Fighting the process will only make it worse, so we ought all to resign ourselves to the best adjustment possible, the smoother the better. What is inevitable, Adams concluded, ought not to be delayed. But it may be asked, if this is the true Adams, why Kirk bothers to include him alongside such men as Burke and Adams' great-grandfather? Brooks Adams, it turns out, did not take his own advice. His convictions rubbed his prejudices the wrong way, making his whole philosophy, in Kirk's opinion, an exercise in irony. "Expansion, consolidation, and dispassionate reception of change, which he pretended to recommend, he really knew to be the poison of everything he honored, and this half-suppressed groan of torment persisted in escaping from him, giving the lie to his theories."[95] World War I and the "unsexing of women," the corruption of the law, destructive taxes, and the general democratic tendency to equalize downward all dismayed Adams: "Social war, or massacre, would seem to be the natural ending of the democratic philosophy."[96] Of course, if that is true, it becomes hard to accept Adams' advice to abandon the past for the sake of peaceful accommodation to such an apocalyptic future. The conservatism of Adams turns out to depend on his contradictions, for the only certainty Kirk finds in Adams is of the dissolution of intellectual energy and freedom as the process of economic expansion continues. The coming American economic supremacy would be accompanied by a social decline that would efface the system that Washington or Jefferson had envisioned, and Brooks Adams counseled acceptance—an acceptance he could not stomach, captive as he was to Marxist economic determinism yet shorn of "the belief that had made the Adams family great: the idea of Providence and Purpose."[97]

Kirk leaves conservatism where he found it at the beginning of the chapter, in dire straits. The cake of custom was not only broken; it was ground underfoot. Under

McKinley and Theodore Roosevelt the nation blundered along the broad way of industrial expansion and moral decay. (Kirk reveals a little personal animosity when he holds up the mass-produced automobile as an example of what unrestrained capitalism can do to traditional ways of life. His scorn for the "mechanical Jacobin" almost drips from the page.) It is a dark day for the defenders of order and tradition; "by the time the First World War ended, true conservatism was nearly extinct in the United States. . . ."[98] Kirk will have to leap the Atlantic again in search of conservatism's banner men.

Chapter Eleven
English Conservatism Adrift: The Twentieth Century

The Conservative party was in a position of near-impregnability after 1895, enjoying the support of powerful interests, including the Whig landed families and Chamberlain's Radicals. The greater part of the rich upper classes and the upper-middle classes were solidly Conservative, and, even better, Britain's imperialism and its popular endorsement had come out in their favor. Disraeli had foreseen the need for colonial resources to match Germany and America, and Lord Salisbury was doing a fine job at the foreign office. The Liberals, the Tories' old nemesis, were weaker, for their part, than they had been in some time, and would splinter further still. They had been infected by socialism but were vacillating over old Liberal policies they had seen dissolve. All their philosophy had been predicated on the fantasy that if all men were only given political power, they would take a constant interest in the affairs of the nation, keep themselves informed, and make intelligent, educated decisions for the good of the whole. When it was proved yet again that most men are not and will not be guided by reason, the Liberals found themselves out of a job.

However, after only a decade, the Conservatives fell from power and would not recover for nearly 80 years. The obvious political causes Kirk lists, but his real attention is fixed on the deeper problems: the decay of Victorian confidence and the swelling influence of the socialists. Simply put, Britain was losing the economic competition with her industrial rivals, and though it was no fault of the Conservatives that British natural advantages were disappearing and that British citizens had been taught to expect constant material improvement and prosperity by the Liberals, they were blamed nonetheless by their constituents in 1906. The revival of the socialists as a vigorous party and their alliance with the Liberals exacerbated the situation. For the first time, a significant Labour (socialist) group sat in Parliament, and before long, Labour would itself outstrip the Liberals, and English politics would be a struggle between conservatives and socialists.

That connoisseur of misery, George Gissing, is discussed in the second section of this chapter. Gissing once resided in the poorest, grimiest sections of London, and so to him Kirk looks to understand the currents of proletarian politics from this time. Gissing knew the poor—he had been one of them, and he knew the socialists because he had given their speeches. It was not long, however, before experience with the socialist agenda and its effects on the working class caused him to repent, and he became an eloquent conservative. The same man who wrote *Workers in the Dawn*, who aspired to be the mouthpiece of the Radicals, examined his folly four years later in *The Unclassed*, writing,

I often amuse myself with taking to pieces of my former self. I was not a conscious hypocrite in those days of violent radicalism, workingman's-club lecturing, and the like; the fault was that I understood myself as yet so imperfectly. That zeal on behalf of the suffering masses was nothing more nor less than disguised zeal on behalf of my own starved passions. I was poor and desperate, life had no pleasures, the future seemed hopeless, yet I was overflowing with vehement desires, every nerve in me was a hunger which cried out to be appeased. I identified myself with the poor and ignorant; I did not make their cause my own, but my cause theirs. I raved for freedom because I was myself in the bondage of unsatisfiable longing.[99]

Now that Gissing had abandoned socialism, he began to speak of *duty*; the only reform possible and really worthwhile was reforming one's character. Gissing saw no shelter from the harsh realities of life on the lowest rung of the economic ladder except that of stoic endurance and self-amendment. In the world of Gissing, the whole duty of man, Kirk relates, "is to stand siege within the fortress of his character."[100] Unlike his socialist counterparts, Gissing believed the only proper channel for real improvement in society was improving the character of the educated and the leaders of society. Unfortunately, he had little hope.

Kirk finds a nagging doubt in Gissing's later thought that the beauty in literature and philosophy would withstand the attack from modern secularism, and that the new collectivism, by whatever name, would fail to erase the variety and individuality that make life tolerable. Instead, his advice to those who would fight the good fight is to cling to what remains of a better world with the tenacity of men over an abyss. The chiefest protection against a fiery end in anarchy, he thought, lay in reconciling the British aristocratic ideal with the "grey-coated multitude." But whether such reconciliation occurs, or is even possible, Kirk gives much the same counsel as Gissing: "Such of us as still are men, then, will hold fast by shaken constitutions and fading beauties so long as there is breath in us."[101]

That rally of the Conservatives at the end of the 19th century was under the guidance of two men, Lord Salisbury and Arthur Balfour, the latter of which is discussed in the third section of this chapter. Balfour was a gentleman of the old school, an aristocratic master of ambiguity and compromise, taming the fervent Radical and industrial interests represented by Joseph Chamberlain to work under conservative principles. Balfour's tactics were restraint, guidance, resistance, defense, diversion, and concession. His practical politics were neatly summed up by the following statement of Saintsbury's: "Fight for it as long as you possibly can consistently with saving as much of it as you possibly can; but stave off the fighting by gradual and insignificant concessions where possible."[102]

Kirk defends Balfour from the blame that was heaped upon him in 1911, when he was practically forced to resign. The Conservatives felt that Balfour was the wrong sort of man for the task at hand now that times had changed, but that was partly their own doing. He struggled "not simply against the altered spirit of the age, but against the altered constitution of his own party."[103] What had happened, in truth, was a shift in the power base of the Conservative ranks. Balfour was a country gentleman, a member of the landed aristocracy, and while they still stood behind the party, it was the manufacturing interests, the urban powers, that were to be the bulk of Conservative support from that point on. Balfour was a worthy leader of the leisured class in their last years of ascendancy, but when those years were gone, his time was past.

Despite Balfour's political fortunes, Kirk notes that his writings are worthy of including him in the pantheon on conservative thinkers. Balfour's philosophical ruminations are contained in four volumes: *A Defense of Philosophic Doubt, The Foundations of Belief, Theism and Humanism,* and *Theism and Thought,* and in them he outlines his skepticism of skepticism. Balfour scoffed at the presumption of "exact" science to claim the only legitimate means of verifying propositions as true or false. If only sensory evidence and physical research is accepted as factual, man will languish in doubt forever—doubt about the most important of all things, first principles. Skepticism of positivism and scientific empiricism led Balfour to theism, to belief in a personal God who takes an active interest in the affairs of men. "The truth of what Coleridge called the Reason, and Newman called the Illative Sense, is what Balfour sets against both naturalistic materialism and anti-Christian idealism."[104] Spiritual truth does not admit of physical proofs, and the man who demands them is not really looking for truth at all. Balfour followed in the footsteps of Burke with such a trust in authority and moral intuition, and, like Burke, he knew how to apply such conservative principles to practical administration, even if some of his larger endeavors were short-sighted. Balfour, "the witty and cultivated voice of traditional Britain,"[105] bowed out gracefully when his defeat came upon him, commenting as he went on the state of the nation—a state of decadence, he said, the loss of an object in life. He had "1914" set into the wrought-iron gate he purchased with a fee for a lecture he had given that same year. It was the year he was proven terrifyingly correct.

This chapter's fourth section describes the works of W. H. Mallock, the author of 27 volumes and a brilliant defender of traditional ways of life. Mallock bent all his talents to showing the ignorant fallacy of the socialist and positivist dream. A country gentleman by birth and a poet by inclination, Mallock made himself a formidable pamphleteer and statistician, determined to defend conservatism on intellectual, even scientific grounds, using the Benthamites' methods against them. His immense contributions to the conservative cause can be divided into his attacks on atheism and socialism.

With *Is Life Worth Living*, Mallock launched a massive broadside at the spirit of positivism which loomed in his beloved England. Its message is simply that morality and happiness cannot subsist without the foundation of supernatural religion. Without moral ends, man will begin his degradation into the beast which always lies close beneath the skin of civilization. And if that is true, the question must be asked: can the claims of orthodox religion be accepted as true, especially in his era that was starry-eyed with science? Kirk answers that the man who venerates his ancestors and cares for his posterity will stand up to defend against "Vandals of the intellect" and show agnostic science itself to be unsound. Regretfully, Kirk does not explain further how Mallock would have them do so.

Far more attention is lavished on Mallock's tremendous undertaking in the field of political economy, a field almost universally shunned by conservatives and dominated by the Liberals, Burke, of course, being a large exception. Mallock knew of the dire need for a thoughtful, conservative reply to the claims of the Liberals and socialists (there was fast becoming little difference between them); no longer could the old verities of tradition, property, and order be wearily put to the task of defense when what was needed was a scientific rebuttal of socialist claims, an organized, systematic reply to Radical doctrines. The supreme issue to be decided by such a work was this: is the idea of social equality true or false? Would society be perfect if only everyone were made equal with everyone else? In *Social Equality and Labour* and *the Popular Welfare* Mallock gives his answer.

Far from being the necessary precondition of social progress and harmony, Mallock shows that throughout history, progress of every sort—economic and cultural—has been the result of the desire of men for *inequality* of condition. Without the possibility of advancement, men of superior ability will have no motivation to use their talents to any degree beyond what is necessary for their own subsistence—why exert oneself if your reward is taken from you and given to those who did nothing? Mallock places the blame for the Marxist failure to see such an obvious truth on their erroneous labor theory of wealth, which holds that labor is the cause of wealth. On the contrary, says Mallock, unaided labor produces a mere subsistence, just enough to survive, if it is not assisted and guided by Ability. The principal motive for wealth is inequality. And, the principal producer of wealth is Ability, the genius and cleverness of men of higher than average talents, without whom the poor would remain in a universally depressed condition. Ability is a natural monopoly, not susceptible of redistribution by legislation, which directs labor, produces inventions, organizes production and distribution, devises methods, and maintains order.[106] Labor without Ability will keep mankind forever plowing the ground when he is not hunting for game. Likewise, the accumulation of capital and the inheritance of property are two very weighty incentives for Ability, allowing great men to pass along the fruits of their labor, rightfully their own, to their descendents, who can use it to produce further wealth and create more jobs in the economy. Mallock uses statistics to prove that from 1800 to 1880 the absolute *and* proportionate wages of the laboring classes rose exponentially, "a progress," Mallock notes, "which the wildest Socialist would never have dreamed of promising."[107] If government is used to take from the wealthy of what belongs to them, ability will be stifled and society will sink into a plain of poverty. Or, as it has been wittily put, if you take from those who have much to give to those who have little, everyone *will* have exactly the same: nothing. There will be no labor-saving devices created, no music written, no art crafted, no medicine discovered, no relief from natural hardships, no diversification of labor, no leisure, no culture, and certainly no progress. With his massive research done, Mallock concludes that civilization depends upon the encouragement, recognition and reward of men of Ability.[108]

In section five Kirk dismisses the few who might be said to represent conservatism in Britain between the two world wars. Men like G.K. Chesterton and Hilaire Belloc were conservative, to be sure, and public figures, to some extent, but they were auxiliaries, Kirk declares, not marshals. Of this ugly time, Kirk says, "it is difficult to write anything worth reading."

Chapter Twelve
Critical Conservatism

The early decades of the 20th century found America blessed with the best literary and philosophical criticism it had ever had, exemplified as that criticism was by the likes of Irving Babbitt and Paul Elmore More, inheritors of the New England tradition, and George Santayana, that Spanish cosmopolitan. Kirk regrets having to pass over other significant conservative figures of the time, among them Albert Jay Nock, the Southern Agrarians, and Ralph Adams Cram, but he finds that the trio he selected were the most important representatives of the American conservative impulse after 1918.

In this first section, Kirk notes that it is ominous to be forced to turn to men of letters to find those who carry the conservative torch, since only their kind remain to carry it, having been abandoned to the task by "a dwindling remnant of old-fashioned philosophical statesmen," who have fled the field. More foreboding still were the social conditions prevalent in this rough-and-tumble era. The rural population continued to decline, as did the vigor of the small towns; industrialism was still gaining strength, upsetting the social order and threatening to dominate the country; a hazy sentimentality and a concrete appetite for power and global expansion dominated; and a dangerous new naturalism advanced by John Dewey, in whom all radical doctrines since 1789 were combined, was growing. In Dewey, the craving of America for power was given "a philosophic mask," the removal of which was the task of the three conservatives to which we now turn.[109]

Section two is devoted to Babbitt, a professor of comparative literature at Harvard and founder of the school of American philosophy he called humanism. Kirk spends considerable time on Babbitt, treating several of his ideas, the first of which is the distinction Babbitt and his fellow humanists made between humanism and humanitarianism. The humanist concerns himself with the higher part of man's nature and the disciplines that can nurture man's spirit, such as philosophy and art, which truly distinguish man from beast. The humanitarian, by contrast, advocates the solution of all man's troubles by physical remedies and Utilitarian methods and pursues a social egalitarianism hostile to "those spiritual essences in man which make possible truly *human life*."[110] In sum, the humanist believes there is such a thing as the life of the spirit and that such a belief is crucial to civilization. The humanitarian denies both claims and therefore also denies that man stands in any need of moral improvement or checks upon his fallen nature. Babbitt and his allies in this chapter, Kirk tells us, agreed that "the saving of civilization is contingent upon the revival of something like the doctrine of original sin."[111]

Babbitt's humanism found its chief expression in *Democracy and Leadership,* which, like all of his works, touches on every point in his system. Published in 1924, the essay came at a time when naturalism like Dewey's was sprouting up like a noxious weed all over the social landscape. Babbitt believed the old bulwarks of prejudice and prescription had collapsed; salvation lay in swaying men to an alternative system of ideas. Against the lie that all man's problems can be solved by material improvement, the humanist must proclaim once more that there is law for man and law for thing—that man, in other words, is a creature with a soul, and therefore must have a purpose that transcends this earthly life. Humanitarians, Babbitt objected, denied the duality (flesh and spirit) of the human experience and omitted the "keystone in the arch of humanity"—the Will. Unique to man, this power, the ability to restrain his appetites, even his reason, is what makes him human.

Having laid the groundwork, Babbitt made his argument—civilization will perish if its lack of true leadership persists. He was convinced:

>...that genuine leadership, good or bad, there will always be, and that democracy becomes a menace to civilization when it seeks to evade the truth...On the appearance of leaders who have recovered in some form the truths of the inner life and repudiated the errors of naturalism may depend the very survival of Western civilization.[112]

The political denial of a moral law can be traced to Machiavelli, and with Hobbes it entered the English political tradition, which has still not recovered from the poison. Society urgently needs political leaders who are willing and able to refute the naturalistic errors of modernity. Only such leaders will be capable of restraining the "tremendous imperialistic instinct" of modern democracy that Babbitt was convinced would plague the world again, if the virtue of humility was not rediscovered. Only such leaders could correct the doctrine of work that had crept in with Francis Bacon and continued by Locke and Marx. Work for them was quantitative and outward, but work as Babbitt conceived it was inner work, the labor of the spirit, and of self-reform. True freedom is the freedom to work in this manner, to satisfy Justice, which Babbitt, following Plato, defined as "doing one's own work or minding one's own business."[113] Society ought to provide the means necessary for men whose work is ethical and spiritual to make themselves ready to lead. Kirk agrees, asserting, "Any real civilization must relieve certain individuals of the necessity for working with their hands, so that they may participate in that leisure which is an indispensable preparation for leadership."[114]

Where are we to discover such leaders, whose great merit must be humility and whose great task nothing less than saving civilization? Neither Babbitt nor Kirk really answer the question, though they are sure that to be a leader a man must possess an ethical center, and he must have the right understanding of work and justice. He must be intellectually serious and morally grave and convinced that men have souls and ought to be treated as spiritual beings. He must, in short, have a strong and upright Will, and he must believe society to be more than a machine and man to be more than a cog. Kirk regrets that Babbitt could not bring himself to treat politics on still higher plane than ethical self-reformation—the plane of grace. Paul Elmore More, however, was a man of faith, and he is discussed next.

Kirk does not discuss More in section three before mentioning his seminal work, *Shelburne Essays*. Eleven volumes in length, the first of which was published in 1904, More's *magnum opus* was consistent in teaching the necessity of the spiritual life to successful earthly life. Men must maintain the spiritual link between one generation and the next. They must not ignore the past and the future, but they will do exactly that without a firm belief in the reality of the transcendent, the supernatural. All this is very much akin to Babbitt's arguments, but More takes a further step into an explicitly theistic realm. Only men with firm religious conviction can resist the modern forces that threaten to overwhelm society—materialism, collectivism, pragmatism, and the rest. Man is responsible for something beyond the grave; there is more than this life.

But Kirk's real interest in More is not for how he echoes Babbitt; it is for his development of the idea of natural aristocracy. In the ninth volume of the *Shelburne Essays, Aristocracy and Justice*, More insists that men need an aristocracy to lead them out of the drift toward a catastrophe that World War I only foreshadowed. Of course, convincing a raw democracy, such as America was in the early 20th century, that it needed an aristocracy to save it from itself was a daunting challenge, to say the least, and one Kirk thinks is still with us today. "To persuade victorious democracy that it must resurrect aristocracy: this is the tremendous practical problem in our politics."[115]

Of course, this aristocracy is quite different from Europe's. It will have no titles, no inherited privilege, no dominion over the nation's wealth. This aristocracy can only be a *natural* aristocracy, so called because it is composed of those who are the best of their community, selected as such and given power. Simply put, More calls for some mechanism or social consciousness that will ensure only the best among us gain power, and Kirk agrees with him. The men who gain the nation's helm are not those who best flatter us or promise the most, but those who are best qualified to pilot the nation. To that end, Kirk declares, our first step ought to be the reformation of higher learning.

Society has been dying at the top. Higher education has been slipping into the abyss of technical training at the expense of preparing the "natural champions of order" to take their place in front. College ought to be where natural leaders can receive a liberal to take their place in front. College ought to be where natural leaders can receive a liberal education, one suited to free men seeking to improve their minds. What is this education, exactly? Kirk quotes Babbitt:

> The scheme of the humanist might be described in a word as a disciplining of the higher faculty of the imagination to the end that the student may behold, as it were in one sublime vision, the whole scale of being in its range from the lowest to the highest under the divine decree of order and subordination, without losing sight of the immutable veracity at the heart of all development, which 'is only the praise and surname of virtue.' This was no new vision, nor has it ever been quite forgotten. It was the whole meaning of religion to Hooker, from whom it passed into all that is best and least ephemeral in the Anglican Church. It was the basis, more modestly expressed, of Blackstone's conception of the British Constitution and of liberty under law. It was the kernel of Burke's theory of statecraft.[116]

"Lacking such an education," Kirk warns, "men have no hold upon the past; they are at the mercy of every wind of doctrine."[117]

Kirk further discusses the principle of Justice, on which such an aristocracy would govern the affairs of state. More denies the sentimental term "social justice" in favor of his own: "the act of right distribution, the giving to each man his due.[118] What is in view here is property, and the right to the same. True social justice is the giving or distribution of property equal to the abilities of the owner, balancing the due part of the superior and inferior classes of society. This theory, of course, is cause and effect of inequality among men, some being more adept at amassing wealth than others, but the right of every man to his own must be inviolable—it is the means of civilization itself. More knew that secure property was essential to the establishment and sustenance of a leisured, aristocratic class such as he looked for—so essential, in fact, that he had no qualms about placing the rights of property above the right to life itself.[119] Without secure property, the church and the university, to say nothing of an aristocracy, are in great peril.

Kirk identifies a second "great phase" of More's contribution to American letters, his study of Christianity and Platonism called *The Greek Tradition*. Kirk does not spend much time on this work, however, beyond providing a few bare facts and commenting that it is the greatest American work of Christian apologetics. More analyzed the dualism of Plato, traced the monism of Stoicism and Epicureanism, and defended the orthodoxy of the Incarnation and the supernatural realm in general. Kirk considers the work to have dealt "a most serious blow to the theological modernism of the 20th century, establishing strongly that premise of metaphysical dualism upon which More's critical and social ideas were built."[120] Kirk believes that, in More, American conservative ideas were reinvigorated and a great blow dealt to the naturalism and humanitarianism rampant at the time. More knew that a belief in God and in the transcendent purpose of man, was a crucial social counterweight to the materialistic greed of natural man, and, unlike Babbitt, he did not draw back from the last step.

In section four we read of George Santayana, the Spanish-born philosopher of conservative bent and urbane style. Santayana's metaphysics were not as orthodox as More's, which is to say that they were not orthodox at all, since he rejected dualism. Kirk defends him as a conservative nonetheless, claiming that he exposed the egoism of the Idealists and the foolishness of pragmatism. He did not believe in any spiritual reality, but he did believe that this natural world has "a spiritual life possible in it" that reaches for a beauty and perfection never quite attained. For all his skepticism, however, Santayana was no enemy of religion; he could not subscribe to the dogmas of the faith, but he had great respect, writes Kirk, for the hope and beauty religion produces. Kirk sees Santayana as a withdrawn philosopher, smiling tolerantly at the flux of the world as he declines to take too active a part in it, content to contemplate the variety of life in his own "grand placidity."[121] But, Kirk tells us, beneath this generous tolerance lies a severe standard by which Santayana judges civilization, which is that a good society is beautiful, a bad society ugly. On this aesthetic ground he built his conservatism.

Santayana was a scourge to liberalism and the innovating impulse it fostered. Kirk relates that once, in a conversation with oil magnate John D. Rockefeller, Santayana happened to mention the population of Spain, whereupon the millionaire commented that his company did not sell enough oil there. In that one sentence Santayana said he saw all the scheme of the monopolist: complete domination of the market, uniformity of production, distribution, and consumption, the triumph of the cheapest—all anathema to the Spaniard. He despised the lust for change that would ruin the world for the sake of efficiency and defended the old order of social harmony and tradition. He believed liberalism was reaching its final, logical culmination—utilitarian collectivism. Liberalism itself, he thought, was merely a loosening of the old order, but it led to the domination of centralized industrialism and the socialist state over the old ways of social hierarchy, property, and family. It was this tendency of liberalism to level down civilization into a cheap and dreary pattern that stoked Santayana's wrath. Such a system degrades the masses, despite its pretenses, and the new mediocre man "becomes a denizen of those slimy quarters, under the shadow of railway bridges, breweries, and gasworks, where the blear lights of a public house peer through the rain at every corner, and offer him the one joy remaining in life."[122] Santayana's words depict his conviction that unrestrained liberalism will reform society to the point that uniformity and equality will grind the soul of social man to a powder beneath the wheel of the industrial machine. "Materialism, confused with tradition, is turned into a sort of religion, and more and more America inclines toward a universal crusade on behalf of this credo of mechanized production and mass consumption."[123] What hope was there, in Santayana's eyes? Kirk says he was inclined to believe that forces, not men, were the real agents of historical change, but Kirk holds out for the power of brave men, lovers of reason and beauty and order, to resist "mechanized monotony" in hopes of preserving in some measure the nobility of mind civilization makes possible.

In section five Kirk chronicles the triumph and embarrassment of liberalism in America following World War I. At first, the war seemed a confirmation of the liberal message, and the three forces of leveling humanitarianism, imperialism, and hedonism gripped the nation. For the first, the income tax and the inheritance tax proved too tempting a tool for the reformers' greedy hands, and it is amazing that the robbing of the propertied class has not gone further. Secondly, Kirk notes the rise of an "insidious and portentous imperialism," one beloved of the humanitarians, which, more than just a military endeavor, was "a resolution that all the world should be induced to embrace American principles and modes of life, founded upon the immense presumption that American society is the final superior product of human ingenuity."[124] And lastly, religion declined into a vague work ethic and an appetite for mass-produced prosperity. Real leadership was gone, the state was in incompetent hands, from Harding to F.D.R., and conservatism found itself in need of revival.

Chapter Thirteen
Conservatives' Promise

In his last chapter Kirk considers the state of conservative ideas in the Western world since the French Revolution. He added this chapter in the 1985 edition of the book, allowing him to take into account the resurgence of conservative feeling in America and Britain in the decade of Reagan and Thatcher. He found that while socialism and Utilitarianism had nearly expired, conservative convictions endured. In America today, he notes, no prominent politician will call himself a socialist. Certainly, since 1789, conservatives have been routed time and again but have not despaired, and there are signs of life in them yet. America is still the home of a robust Christianity, and so the basis of any conservative order, religious sanction, remains somewhat secure. The federal constitution has stood the test of time as the most effective conservative document in political history, despite grievous abuse; the balance of power still operates, and there is no real movement for revolution. Likewise, the British constitution still provides for a bicameral Parliament with the Crown presiding, the monarchy still respected by all factions.[125] Private property, too, still stands secure, if embattled, in both countries, and Kirk believes that even tradition and ancient custom eke out an existence today, not entirely destroyed by the mass media and industrialized uniformity.

The most serious injuries sustained by conservatism are the decline of leadership and the problem of reconciling individualism with the sense of community necessary to society. Kirk is convinced that conservatism's greatest task in our time is the provision of leaders who can strike a balance between the isolation of single persons in a group, a lonely crowd, and the myth of the unified, all-powerful state. Men must fall in love again with what Burke called the "little platoon," the local voluntary associations and institutions that draw men out of them and engage them in the community while providing a buffer between men and the state. It remains to be seen, says Kirk, whether conservatives can manage to restore these ideals, so critical to social stability and felicity. The alternative is a slide into a collectivism without any of the nice liberal trappings.

If conservatism is to resist the advent of a new statism of Orwellian dimensions, a "super-bureaucracy" of managers, experts, and statisticians, "the colossal state created for its own sake," then we must attend to certain pressing concerns, certain primary difficulties of the social order, which Kirk identifies. If we are to fend off Big Brother government, we must affirm the idea of normality in society; we must hold forth standards to which men may repair. Man is not perfectible, he says, "but he may achieve a tolerable degree of order, justice, and freedom," and he must, by humane study, ascertain those norms and teach them to the statesman.[126]

First among the concerns of modern conservatives is the regeneration of spirit and character, by which Kirk means the renewal of religious ideals, the one sure foundation for a life worth living. Kirk cautions that political Christianity, in which God is a means to an end, will not suffice. Rather, spiritual renewal must be done for its own sake.

The conservative is also concerned, as Kirk has mentioned before, with the problem of leadership, which has two aspects: the preservation of reverence, order, discipline, and class and the cleansing of our system of education, so that it can become liberal in the best sense of that word. "Only just leadership can redeem society from the mastery of the ignoble elite."[127]

Third, the phenomenon of the proletariat should receive conservatives' attention. Somehow, modern men must find hope and status, a place of satisfaction and belonging, links with the past and expectations for the future, and duty as well as right, if it is to be redeemed from social boredom and the temptation to use the power of the state to redistribute wealth in its favor.

The conservative is concerned with resistance to ideology. He endeavors to restore true political philosophy, insisting that we cannot make a Heaven of earth, though we can certainly make a Hell of it through the utopian fancies of ideology. We must learn our limits and by prudent consideration make the best we can of a world where sinful men live with each other.

As mentioned above, the conservative must seek after the recovery of true community, local energies and cooperation, voluntary endeavor, and social diversity. The decay of this sort of community creates crime and poverty, whole classes being displaced out of cities in the name of "urban renewal," and small towns and rural living dwindling to starvation by economic practices blind to whatever lacks a price tag. Kirk believes urban riots and crime can be traced back to the destruction of community, and so conservatives should talk of the need for roots and community, not mass welfare.

In section three Kirk discusses the state of conservatism in America since 1950 and contrasts the scholar to the intellectual. In that year, Lionel Trilling denied that conservatism still lived as an intellectual tradition in America. Yet, scarcely had he written such a charge, Kirk says, before a powerful resurgence of traditional conservative thought began to make itself felt. He estimates that since 1950 some 200 books of serious conservative thought have been published, in addition to a welter of periodicals and essays, so many, in fact, as to prevent Kirk from listing names in this last edition of his book.[128] The men responsible for this renaissance were scholars, Kirk insists, not the liberal substitute—the intellectual.

Kirk traces the term "intellectual" back to its roots in the Enlightenment, not exactly a conservative event. By about 1950, liberal intellectuals seemed to have the run of the ship, but in ensuing years, conservative thinkers demonstrated that self-styled "intellectuals" had no monopoly on intellectual power. Those thinkers had no wish to be called by a name that, in 20th-century usage, was associated with Marxist jargon to refer to a body of schooled and highly rational persons opposed to established social institutions. Beginning in the 1920s, a number of educated Americans and Englishmen began to call themselves intellectuals, and the term gradually came to be identified with secular ideology, at a time when the nation seemed to forsake all but profit. "'Intellectuals' appeared in America when the works of the mind began to lose ground in public influence."[129]

And so it was that Trilling could not find any conservative intellectuals in 1950. They would not have the title. But there was an older model, Kirk reminds us, of the man of reflection and learning, a man not alienated from his cultural heritage—the scholar. He reaches back to 1843 for Brownson's definition:

> I understand by scholar no mere pedant, dilettante, literary epicure or dandy; but a serious, robust, full-grown man; who feels that life is a serious affair, and that he has a serious part to act in its eventful drama; and must therefore do his best to act well his part, so as to leave behind him, in the good he has done, a grateful remembrance of his having been. He may be a theologian, a politician, a naturalist, a poet, a moralist, or a metaphysician; but whichever or whatever he is, he is it with all his heart and soul, with high, noble—in one word, *religious* aims and aspirations.[130]

In this Cold War era, the public began to become fertile ground for conservative ideas, looking for an alternative to the centralization of Communist ideology. In the social disciplines, Kirk writes, a lively minority of conservative scholars made itself known, and those scholars argued that their disciplines could achieve much if they labored for conservative ideals, ideals Kirk is generous enough to list.

First, scholars in the human sciences ought to address themselves to the concerns of genuine community, by which he means local and voluntary community, as opposed to promoting more egalitarian collectivism. Rally the little platoons, is the cry.

Second, those scholars should turn their attentions to private associations, rather than seek to expand the unitary state. Kirk calls for moral imagination, the admission of religious belief, the denial of "value-free science," and the affirmation of the existence of a moral order.

Third, it would be well for each of them to renew the old definition of justice, and to recognize diversity as a good rather than seek the standardization of life. They ought to admit the virtues, Kirk thinks, of order and class, and encourage the growth of talented leadership.

Lastly, good conservative scholars and scientists should speak up for permanence, as against change for its own sake, and recognize man's deep need for continuity and tradition. "If the need of the eighteenth century was for emancipation, the need of the twentieth is for roots."[131] Only when such studies are undertaken by scholars and absorbed by the politicians can the disorders of this age be intelligently confronted and their remedies applied.

One shining example of such a conservative study of social ailments is Robert Nisbet's *The Quest for Community*, published in 1953. Nisbet believed the paramount moral problem of our time is the problem of community lost and regained. The decay of family and guilds, the retreat of local government before the central state, and the sad condition of religious belief—in short, the destruction of traditional society—has produced the Lonely Crowd, a mass of individuals together, but apart. It is an aggregate of anonymous faces, a swarm of strangers on a city street, in the subway, or at the store. Individuals have been set free from family, religion, and local political community to such an extent that they have become islands in an ocean of islands. In such an environment, Nisbet feared, collectivism would appeal as a source of certitude and membership, of belonging and security. People will grasp at purpose wherever they can find it. The most powerful factor in the decline of such community was the rise of the modern state, the triumph of which Nisbet thought to be the single most decisive influence on Western social organization. Men have sought in the vast, impersonal state a replacement for all the old associations they but dimly sense they have lost.

The 19th century, said Nisbet, was the century of the political masses' emergence, thanks to industrialism and liberalism. The masses became enamored of the state for its power to grant them benefits and deliver them from misery and injustice. And so the omnipotent state, in turn, found in the new masses the perfect instrument for its rise to greater power. The modern total state is a popular creation, and a monument to the myopia of liberals. They assumed man was sufficient unto himself, and so gave political power to all, but individualism was overwhelmed by the loneliness of man, and therefore by the masses' total state.

What to do, then, to combat such dire developments? Kirk and Nisbet claim that we must remember that the will is free, and so the centralization of power is *not* the unavoidable direction of history. We must check the usurpation of power with a new *laissez-faire*, within which autonomous groups, not individuals, may prosper. The basic social unit will be the group: the family, the local community, the church, the college, the profession, the trade union, and so forth. Diversity, not union, will be the goal, a plurality of associations and responsibilities within which men may find purpose and be sheltered from an overweening state. The freedom of the person, within these spheres, will be jealously guarded.

In section four Kirk considers the poets, allies of the scholars in cause of conservatism. Poets and their moral imagination can help to restore a living faith in the lonely crowd, and can help remind man that life has ends. Chief among such poets for Kirk is T.S. Eliot, whose whole endeavor, Kirk writes, was to point the way to order in the soul and society. Eliot, in *The Idea of a Christian Society and Notes towards the Definition of Culture,* defended the beliefs and customs that nurture civilization and fought back against the industrialism that created mobs of homeless men and women. Eliot, Kirk tells us, believed in class, order, and the permanent things of life. He distrusted the new elite, recruited as it was from the masses and trained in spiritually lifeless state schools in secular collectivism and unrestrained by notions of honor, duty, or tradition. They are administrators; what is needed is an aristocracy.

But rather than elaborate on Eliot's arguments, Kirk concludes his mighty work by holding him up as an example of a conservative poet's role as a guide in the restoration of traditional society: "It has been a chief purpose of good poetry to reinterpret and vindicate the norms of human existence." Poets can spark the imagination to a new love for the old beauties, the traditional orders and ways of life, and the wisdom and majesty of the past. Men like Milton, Dryden, Swift, Pope, Johnson, Coleridge, Yeats, and Frost were all conservators of the permanent things, of custom and continuity and veneration. Kirk follows in their footsteps, waxing eloquent in his hope for conservatism's success and his aspersion for innovators:

> Nothing is but thinking makes it so. If men of affairs can rise to the summons of the poets, the norms of culture and politics may endure despite the follies of the time. The individual is foolish; but the species is wise; and so the thinking conservative appeals to what Chesterton called "the democracy of the dead." Against the hubris of the ruthless innovator, the conservative of imagination pronounces Cupid's curse: "They that do chance old love for new, Pray gods they change for worse."[132]

Endnotes

1. Russell Kirk, *The Conservative Mind*, Seventh Revised Edition. Washington, DC: Regnery (1985), p. 23.
2. Ibid, p. 29.
3. Ibid, p. 31.
4. Ibid, p. 33.
5. Ibid, p. 35.
6. Ibid, p. 42.
7. Ibid, p. 44.
8. Ibid, p. 45.
9. Ibid, p. 61.
10. Ibid.
11. Ibid, p. 62 f.
12. Ibid, p. 64.
13. Ibid, p. 65.
14. Ibid, p. 74.
15. Ibid, p. 76.
16. Ibid, p. 77.
17. Ibid, p. 80.
18. Ibid, p. 83.
19. Ibid, pp. 83-84.
20. Ibid, p. 84.
21. Ibid, p. 85.
22. Ibid, p. 86.
23. Ibid, p. 92.
24. See C.S. Lewis, *The Abolition of Man.* San Franciso: Harper (March 2001) ; and *That Hideous Strength.* Princeton, NJ: Scribner (May 6, 2003).
25. Kirk, p. 99.
26. Ibid, p. 100.
27. Ibid, p. 102.
28. Ibid, p. 111.
29. Ibid, p. 117.
30. Ibid, p. 119.
31. Ibid, p. 126.
32. Ibid, p. 129.
33. Ibid, p. 130.

34. A small territory represented by a member of Parliament, something akin to an American state or county, though of varying size and population.
35. Ibid, p. 133.
36. Ibid, p. 134.
37. Ibid, p. 138.
38. Ibid, p. 141.
39. Ibid, p. 157.
40. Ibid, p. 161.
41. Ibid, p. 164.
42. Ibid, p. 165.
43. Ibid, p. 169.
44. Ibid, p. 175.
45. Ibid, p. 175 f.
46. Ibid, p. 179.
47. Ibid, p. 181.
48. Ibid, p. 184.
49. Ibid, p. 194.
50. Ibid, p. 196.
51. Ibid, p. 204.
52. Ibid, p. 207.
53. Ibid, p. 209.
54. Ibid, p. 211.
55. Ibid, p. 219 f.
56. Ibid, p. 224.
57. Ibid, p. 226.
58. Ibid, p. 230.
59. Ibid, p. 236.
60. Ibid, p. 238.
61. Ibid, p. 239.
62. Ibid.
63. Ibid, p. 241.
64. Ibid, p. 242.
65. Ibid, p. 244.
66. Ibid, p. 247.
67. Ibid, p. 249.
68. Ibid, p. 251.
69. Ibid, p. 255.

70. Ibid, p. 264.

71. Ibid, p. 269.

72. Ibid, p. 273.

73. Ibid, p. 274.

74. Ibid, p. 285.

75. Ibid.

76. Ibid, p. 290.

77. Ibid, p. 291.

78. Ibid, p. 294.

79. Ibid, p. 307 f.

80. Ibid, p. 309.

81. Ibid, p. 310.

82. Ibid, p. 321.

83. Ibid, p. 325.

84. Ibid, p. 339 f.

85. Ibid, p. 343.

86. Ibid, p. 344.

87. Ibid, p. 351.

88. Ibid, p. 357.

89. Ibid, p. 359.

90. Ibid, p. 361.

91. Ibid, p. 363.

92. Ibid, p. 365.

93. Ibid, p. 369.

94. Ibid.

95. Ibid, p. 370.

96. Ibid, p. 371.

97. Ibid, p. 372.

98. Ibid, p. 373.

99. Ibid, p. 382.

100. Ibid, p. 383.

101. Ibid, p. 387.

102. Ibid, p. 389.

103. Ibid.

104. Ibid, p. 392.

105. Ibid, p. 394.

106. Ibid, p. 404.

107. Ibid, p. 405.

108. Ibid, p. 406.

109. Ibid, p. 419.

110. Ibid, p. 421.

111. Ibid.

112. Ibid, p. 423 f.

113. Ibid, p. 427.

114. Ibid.

115. Ibid, p. 435.

116. Ibid, p. 436.

117. Ibid. The reader will note that this sort of education is not dissimilar to what Newman, among others, recommended. For more on Kirk's views of higher education in this country, see his *Decadence and Renewal in the Higher Learning.*

118. Ibid, p. 437.

119. Ibid, p. 438.

120. Ibid, p. 441.

121. Ibid, p. 445.

122. Ibid, p. 448.

123. Ibid, p. 451 f.

124. Ibid, p. 454. The parallels that could be drawn to recent American policy are startling.

125. Kirk would very likely be much grieved were he alive today to learn of the mauling of the House of Lords in this new century. The Labour party decimated the ancient institution in an act of breathtaking arrogance, forcing the members of that august body to defend their own individual place their by writing a paper! Only some ninety-odd lords were allowed to remain.

126. Ibid, p. 472.

127. Ibid.

128. Ibid, p. 476.

129. Ibid, p. 479.

130. Ibid, p. 479 f.

131. Ibid, p. 482.

132. Ibid, p. 500 f.

Printed in the USA
CPSIA information can be obtained
at www.ICGtesting.com
LVHW091136240124
769840LV00004B/122